HERMES
THE
THIEF

HERMES THE THIEF

THE EVOLUTION OF A MYTH

NORMAN O. BROWN

VINTAGE BOOKS

A DIVISION OF RANDOM HOUSE

NEW YORK

PREFACE

This study of the Greek god Hermes explores the hypothesis that the interrelation of Greek mythology and Greek history is much closer than has generally been recognized. Such a hypothesis seems almost inescapable in the face of the radical transformation that the attributes and personality of Hermes underwent during the archaic period of Greek history. What I have sought to do here is to correlate these changes with the revolution in economic techniques, social organization, and modes of thought that took place in Athens between the Homeric age and the fifth century B.C. Such a correlation, I submit, casts new light on the mythology of Hermes, and especially on the *Homeric Hymn to Hermes*.

The study was conceived six years ago in the genial atmosphere of the University of Wisconsin. The ideas in it have benefited from the stimulus of association with members of its faculty, especially Professors A. D. Winspear, Walter R. Agard, Charles F. Edson, Howard Becker, and the late William Ellery Leonard. Their exposition has benefited—to an extent which only those who know her work will appreciate—from the searching criticism and constructive assistance of Miss Livia Appel, managing editor of the University of Wisconsin Press. I am also indebted for advice and criticism to the late Professor W. A. Oldfather of the University of Illinois and Professors Arthur D. Nock and Sterling Dow of Harvard University. In addition, Professor Homer A. Thompson of the University of Toronto was good enough to give me the benefit of his judgment on certain problems connected with the archaeology of the altar of the Twelve Gods in the Athenian agora.

It need scarcely be added that none of these persons bears the slightest responsibility for any of the conclusions presented.

1947   N. O. B.

This Vintage edition does not represent a revision but a reissue of the author's first work, published in 1947, for many years out of print and unobtainable.

May 1969   N. O. B.

CONTENTS

HERMES
THE
THIEF

CHAPTER

1

TRIBAL MYTHS

In Greek mythology each of the gods figures in a bewildering variety of roles. Hermes is not only the
Thief, but also the Shepherd, the Craftsman, the Herald, the Musician, the Athlete, and the Merchant.
Scholars have usually explained Hermes the Thief as a
derivative of Hermes the Shepherd. According to this
view, the *Homeric Hymn to Hermes,* the story of the
infant Hermes' theft of the cattle of his elder brother
Apollo, represents the original core of the mythology of
Hermes, and reflects the primitive mores of Greek pastoral tribes. In early Greece, according to the historian
Thucydides, plundering expeditions against neighbors
were a widespread and reputable practice, and survived as such even in his own day in the more backward regions. Arcadia, Hermes' birthplace and the
scene of the *Homeric Hymn,* was a land preeminently
pastoral in its economy and rude in its manners. On
these grounds it has very plausibly been concluded

that the institution of cattle-raiding gave rise to the
myth of Hermes the cattle-thief, just as it gave rise to
other myths of cattle-raiding divinities, notably Heracles. Subsequently Hermes· the cattle-thief, adopted
as their patron god by thieves in general, became
Hermes the Thief.[1]

This interpretation is, however, open to a number of
objections. Its fundamental weakness is the assumption
that the *Homeric Hymn* gives us the original core of
the mythology of Hermes. A closer study of the inter-
nal characteristics of the *Hymn*, as we shall see in a
later chapter, leads to the conclusion that it is the
product of a more advanced culture than the primitive
pastoral, and hence cannot be accepted as direct evidence of an original connection between Hermes the
Thief and that earlier culture. In the second place, the
support which the theory derives from the abundant
evidence outside the *Hymn* that Hermes was a patron
god of the pastoral life is vitiated by the fact that it is
only in the particular myth recounted in the *Hymn*
that Hermes is connected with cattle; his pastoral functions, in both myth and ritual, are otherwise restricted
to the protection of sheep.[2] In view of this discrep-

[1] Nilsson, *Greek Popular Religion*, 9; Eitrem, in Pauly-
Wissowa, *Real-Encyclopädie, s.v.* "Hermes," VIII.776; Wilamowitz, *Glaube der Hellenen*, I, 166; Radermacher, *Homerische
Hermeshymnus*, 219–222; Glotz, *Solidarité de la famille dans le
droit criminel en Grèce*, 198–201; Thucydides, I.5.

[2] The epithets applied to Hermes in rituals include "Bearer of
Rams" (Pausanias, IX.22.1) and "Protector of Sheep" (*ibid.*,
IX.34.3); there is none that implies a similar relation to cattle.
Cattle do not appear in Eitrem's list of some twenty animals
connected with Hermes (Pauly-Wissowa, VIII.757–759). The
ox appears as the sacrificial animal in the rituals of Hermes in
only three instances, none of which is a ritual devoted to
Hermes in his capacity as pastoral god (*ibid.*, 836). For these
three instances, see the *Hymn*, 115–137; Plutarch, *Aristides*,
21; and Farnell, *Cults of the Greek States*, Vol. V, p. 74, ref.
85e. Even the *Hymn* itself bears witness to the fact that
Hermes is shepherd rather than neatherd: in line 314, in the
middle of the narrative of the theft of the cattle, he is called

ancy, the *Hymn* cannot be regarded as a simple reflection of the behavior of the god's worshippers. In the third place, the theory neglects other myths of Hermes the Thief, which are more important as evidence for the origin of the epithet than the cattle-stealing episode in the *Hymn*. The *Hymn* is universally recognized to be no older than the seventh century B.C.; in the oldest stratum of Greek mythology—the *Iliad* and the *Odyssey*, and Hesiod's *Works and Days* and *Theogony* —where Hermes does appear as thief, it is not as cattle-thief.

If cattle-raiding is the basis of the concept of Hermes as thief, it is strange that in describing the great age of cattle-raiding, Homer, who was also familiar with Hermes as thief, should have failed to connect the two. His failure to do so might have been accidental, but in the absence of evidence to the contrary, one naturally concludes that in the Homeric age Hermes as thief was not thought of as cattle-thief. In fact, a closer study of the institution of cattle-raiding makes this conclusion mandatory. Cattle-raiding, as depicted in Homer, was a public enterprise, led by the kings and participated in by the whole people. It is described as a war—a resort to force, and open force.[3] The institution appears to have been a common heritage of all the Indo-European peoples and to have had everywhere the same general characteristics. To cite one illustrative detail: the Sanskrit word for "war" means literally "desire for more cows." Coexistent with this institution of warlike plundering, or *robbery*, and terminologically distinguished from it in the Indo-European languages,

---

"Shepherd" (οἰοπόλος) without any dramatic justification. As we shall see, it is because he is a god of the mountain wasteland that Hermes watches over the sheep who graze there and not over cattle, which do not venture so far up.

[3] *Iliad*, 11.684 (πόλεμος); cf. Buchholz, *Homerische Realien*, II, 304–305.

was another type of appropriation, called *theft*. *Theft*
is appropriation by stealth; *robbery* is open and forcible appropriation.[4] In Greek law the terms force and
fraud, robbery and theft, are standard antitheses.
Cattle-raiding, of course, belonged to the category of
robbery.[5]

Once this distinction has been made, there can be
no doubt that the practices associated with Hermes
are *theft,* not *robbery.* The Greek terms which embody
the antithesis between the two are κλοπή, "theft," as
opposed to ἁρπαγή, "robbery"; and βία, "force," as opposed to δόλος, "fraud" or "trickery." The terms most
frequently used to characterize Hermes' thieving are
words of the same root as κλοπή; in the earliest literary
evidence, Homer and Hesiod, words of this root are
used exclusively. In the rituals of Hermes the only epithet expressing this side of the god's nature is δόλιος,
"tricky"; the only ritual which enacted the behavior of
the god was the one performed at the festival of Hermes at Samos, at which there was general license to
steal (κλέπτειν).[6]

Equally characteristic of the thief, as opposed to the
robber, are the actions credited to Hermes in the *Iliad*
and the *Odyssey.* Because the gods do not care to risk
an open attack on the dangerous giants, it falls to
Hermes to steal Ares out of the brazen pot where Otus
and Ephialtes have imprisoned him. On another occasion the gods suggest that Hermes steal Hector's body
away from Achilles because it must be done without
the latter's knowledge. Upon Autolycus, who was ad-

---

[4] Schrader, *Reallexikon der indogermanischen Altertumskunde,*
s.v. "Raub" (II, 212–213), "Viehzucht" (II, 603), and "Diebstahl" (I, 193).

[5] See Ebeling, *Lexicon Homericum, s.v.* ἀμφαδόν; Plato, *Laws,*
941B. The Laconian dialect substituted for the usual Greek
word for "raiders," λησταί, the term "force-thieves" (ἴσφωρες);
see Hesychius, *s.v.* ἴσφωρες.

[6] Pausanias, VII.27.1; Plutarch, *Greek Questions,* 55.

dicted to housebreaking—an enterprise which, according to the *Homeric Hymn to Hermes*, was carried on by night, that is to say by stealth—Hermes bestowed the gift of "stealthiness." In a fragment of poetry attributed to Hesiod, Autolycus' success is attributed to his ability to conceal stolen property: "whatever he took in his hands he made invisible." [7]

The distinction between theft and robbery appears not only as a distinction between terms, and between modes of action, but also as a distinction between types of human beings: habitual stealing produces the cunning trickster, habitual robbery the fighting hero. The typical cattle-raider of Greek mythology is Heracles, that embodiment of the ideal of carrying a big stick and talking loudly. Hermes is just the opposite type; the whole emphasis in the mythology of Hermes is on mental skill or cunning, as opposed to physical prowess.[8]

The *Homeric Hymn to Hermes* and other versions of the same myth do depict Hermes as cattle-raider. One can only conclude, therefore, that the *Hymn*, inasmuch as it ignores a distinction valid in Homer and Hesiod, and consistently applied by them to Hermes, represents a later stage in the mythology of Hermes. Even so, the *Hymn* contains numerous indications that Hermes is the hero of *stealthy* appropriation. Side by side with occasional terminology suitable to the raider appear terms suitable only to the thief. The cattle-raid described in the *Hymn* is not the usual resort to open force, but a peculiarly stealthy operation. There is no more incisive delineation of the contrast between the cunning trickster and the fighting hero than in the

[7] *Iliad,* 5.390; 24.24, 109; *Odyssey,* 19.395–397; cf. *Iliad,* 10.266–267; *Hymn,* 283–284; Hesiod, Frg. 112 (Rzach).

[8] Wilamowitz, *Glaube der Hellenen,* I, 163–164. Odysseus is indeed a fighter who is also "wily," but his tricks are stratagems of war, and were the gift not of Hermes but of Athena; see *Odyssey,* 13.290–300.

Hymn, where Hermes, a helpless infant relying only on his phenomenal cunning, challenges Apollo, the embodiment of physical power and the majesty of established authority.[9]

In view of this distinction between theft and robbery, it may seem plausible to conclude that the mythology of Hermes the Thief is adequately explained by the existence of the institution of theft. And the myths thus far considered can be explained in this way; but there are others.

When the Greek tragedians describe Hermes as "tricky" or as "the trickster," they have in mind not a patron of theft or any other type of misappropriation, but a patron of stealthy action in general. In Aeschylus' *Choephoroi* Hermes is invoked to help Orestes stealthily murder Clytemnestra; in Sophocles' *Philoctetes* he is invoked to aid Odysseus in tricking Philoctetes into joining the Greeks against the Trojans; in Euripides' *Rhesus* he is invoked to aid Dolon in his expedition to spy on the Greek army.[10]

This concept of Hermes as the patron of stealthy action is already present in the oldest stratum of Greek mythology. He has this function in the *Iliad* when, at the behest of Zeus, he steals Priam through the camp of the Greeks, "unseen and unnoticed," to Achilles.[11]

A special kind of stealthy or guileful action is attributed to Hermes in Homer's description of the gift he bestowed on Autolycus. That gift was not merely "stealthiness"; it was "stealthiness and skill at the oath." "Skill at the oath" means guile or cunning in the use of the oath and derives from the primitive idea that an oath was binding only in its literal sense; a cunning person might legitimately manipulate it in order to de-

---

[9] See lines 13, 66–67, 76–78, 155, 162, 175, 235–292, 319, 405, 413, 436, 446, 463, 514, 577.

[10] Hermes δόλιος: Aeschylus, *Choephoroi,* 726; Sophocles, *Philoctetes,* 133; Euripides, *Rhesus,* 216–217.

[11] *Iliad,* 24.337.

ceive, as occurs often enough in Greek mythology. In
the *Homeric Hymn,* when Hermes uses just such an
oath to deny that he has stolen Apollo's cattle, he is
said to show "good skill." [12]

Hermes is the patron of another special kind of
trickery—the trickery involved in sexual seduction—in
Hesiod's myth of Pandora, the Greek Eve, "the source
of all our woe." Determined to wreak vengeance on
humanity because Prometheus had stolen fire from
heaven and given it to mankind, Zeus ordered Hephaestus to fashion Pandora out of clay, and others of
the gods to equip her with the gifts that each had to
bestow. Hermes' gift was "lies and deceitful words and
a stealthy disposition." Hesiod, who was no less a
misogynist than the authors of *Genesis* III and *Paradise Lost,* imputes to Pandora traits which he sees in
womankind. Exactly what he means by the "stealthy
disposition" we shall consider presently; the first part
of the line is in any case a clear allusion to what we
sometimes call "feminine wiles." [13]

These passages, which ascribe to Hermes various
types of trickery, none of them reducible to theft, raise
a new question: is Hermes the Thief the prototype,
from which, by extension and analogy, the Trickster
was derived? Or is the notion of trickery the fundamental one, and theft merely a specific manifestation
of it?

Let us first examine the relation between the two
notions. In modern society theft and trickery are
clearly distinguished. Primitive peoples, however, do

[12] *Odyssey,* 19.396; *Hymn,* 379–380, 389–390. Surely it is a
mistake to see in this manipulation of the oath evidence of sophistication and of waning faith in the power of the oath, as do
Hirzel (*Der Eid,* 43) and Latte (*Heiliges Recht,* 37–38). The
effectiveness of "trickery in the oath" depends on the faith of
both parties in the binding power of the magic words of the oath
formula.
[13] Hesiod, *Works and Days,* 78.

not make the distinction, which probably did not
emerge until the establishment of a legal code empha-
sizing the property rights of the individual.[14] In the
English language the ambiguity in the root of the
word "stealth," which does not necessarily imply stealing, seems to be a vestige of a time when the two
notions were not clearly distinguished. In the Greek
language the characteristic terms applied to Hermes as
thief are derivatives of κλέπτειν, which in fifth-century
Athens meant what "theft" means to us. But in Homeric Greek the root had two well-established mean-
ings: "to remove secretly" and, more frequently, "to
deceive." Even the first meaning does not correspond
to our "theft," since it does not necessarily imply the
violation of property rights. The original meaning of
the root was "secret action," a meaning that is preserved in some Homeric phrases and in some archaistic
usages of the Greek tragedians. Inasmuch as in the
Homeric period no clear-cut distinction was made between theft and trickery, the original Hermes can with
accuracy only be called the Trickster, or, if an English
word which has some of the ambiguity of the Greek
is preferred, the "stealthy." [15]

In the light of this conclusion, the usual interpreta-

[14] Thurnwald, in Ebert, Reallexikon der Vorgeschichte, s.v.
"Diebstahl," II, 390–392.

[15] Ebeling, Lexicon Homericum, s.v. κλέπτω, κλέπτης, κλεπ-
τοσύνη, κλόπιος, ἐπίκλοπος, ὑποκλοπέομαι, ἐκκλέπτω; Boisacq,
Dictionnaire étymologique de la langue grecque, s.v. κλέπτω;
Sophocles, Electra, 37, Ajax, 188. In Homer, besides Odyssey,
19.396, which is discussed below, the only disputable passage
is Iliad, 3.11, where it is said that a fog is "better than night
itself for the κλέπτης." The word is always translated "thief";
but the alternative translation, "trickster," is possible in relation
to the context, and therefore preferable. With κλέπτω compare
φηλήτης, which is applied to Hermes in the Homeric Hymn
in the sense of "thief," but which is used by Hesiod in the sense
of "trickster," and which is of the same root as the Latin fallo,
"deceive"; cf. Hymn, 67, 159, 175, 214, 292; Hesiod, Works and
Days, 375 (discussed below); Boisacq, s.v. φηλήτης.

tions of some of the myths cited above must be modified. Hermes' release of Ares and his removal of Hector's body are not acts of theft, but merely stealthy
actions. Hermes' gift to Autolycus, "stealthiness and
skill at the oath," does not mean skill at stealing and at
the oath, but skill at trickery in general and at tricky
oaths in particular. And what is the "stealthy disposition" that Hermes gave to Pandora? The usual translation is "thievish disposition." But Pandora commits no
theft, and no satisfactory reason has been given why
Hesiod should accuse womankind of thievishness. The
alternative meaning of "tricky" or "guileful" is entirely
congruous: a "guileful disposition" accords with the
"lies and deceitful words" with which Hesiod couples
it; it is the *guiles* of women that he denounces in another passage which is a perfect commentary on
Hermes' gift to Pandora—"Let no strutting dame de-
lude your mind, flattering you with deceitful words,
trying to soften your manhood; he who puts his trust
in woman, puts his trust in tricksters." [16]

To trace the concept of Hermes as thief back to an
earlier concept of Hermes as trickster does not, of
course, explain the latter. Although the trickster-god is
common in the mythology of primitive peoples, its significance has not been agreed upon. Why should trickery have a divine patron? A study of the Greek trickster-god may throw light on the problem.

A review of the mythology of Hermes the Trickster
shows that his trickery is never represented as a ra-
tional device, but as a manifestation of magical power.

[16] *Odyssey*, 19.396, κλεπτοσύνῃ θ' ὅρκῳ τε; Hesiod, *Works and
Days*, 78, ἐπίκλοπον ἦθος; Theognis (line 965) borrows the
phrase from this passage in Hesiod and uses it in the sense of
"guileful disposition." Hesiod, *op. cit.*, 373–375, where the word
translated "tricksters" is φηλήτῃσι; see also note 15 above. The
passage in the *Theogony* (lines 590–612) where Hesiod compares women to drones does not support the translation "thievish
disposition," since "thievishness" would be an impossibly ellip-
tical metaphor for "laziness."

Even in the myth of the cattle theft, in which Hermes
is thief rather than trickster, his success at stealing is
attributed to magic. To get back into his home unob-
served he transforms himself into a mist and passes
through the keyhole. To hide his footprints he invents
shoes which are "unspeakable, unthinkable, marvel-
lous," and which leave tracks described as "the work of
a mighty demon." He prevents the dogs from barking
by putting them to sleep, no doubt by the aid of that
rod of his with which, according to the *Iliad*, "he
charms men's eyes to sleep." [17]

In this story Hermes uses magic to commit a successful theft. Even in the twentieth century thieves have
been known to seek to supplement their technique
with magic. In ancient India, according to a recent
study, thieves used charms of three main types: charms
to put the watch to sleep, charms to break locks, and
charms to make themselves invisible; Hermes too uses
all these types of magic.[18]

[17] *Hymn*, 80, 146–147, 343; cf. 413. The incident of putting
the dogs to sleep is told in the version of Antoninus Liberalis,
Metamorphoses, 23, which is based on the Hesiodic version; see
Holland, "Battos," *Rheinisches Museum*, 75 (1926):156. The
Hymn merely states that the dogs did not bark, an abridgment
which suggests a declining interest in magic and therefore makes
all the more significant the instances of it that do occur in the
Hymn; see Kuiper, "De discrepantiis Hymni Homerici in Mercurium," *Mnemosyne*, n.s., 38 (1910): 35. Hipponax (Frg. 4,
Diehl), treating the matter with Aristophanic realism, calls
Hermes "dog-throttler." For Hermes' rod, see *Iliad*, 24.343
(ὄμματα θέλγει); for a similar myth of Hermes putting dogs to
sleep, see the myth of Io (Preller-Robert, I, 385–387; Wilamowitz, *Glaube der Hellenen*, I, 163). Hermes' power to put to
sleep was invoked in the ritual of pouring the last libation to him
at the end of a banquet; see *Odyssey*, 7.137; Preller-Robert, I,
404.
[18] H. Bächtold-Stäubli, *Handwörterbuch des deutschen Aberglaubens, s.v.* "Dieb"; M. Bloomfield, "The Art of Stealing in
Hindu Fiction," *American Journal of Philology*, 44(1923):118–
120. Nilsson (*Greek Popular Religion*, 9) supports the theory
that the *Hymn* reflects the mentality of primitive cattle-thieves
by comparing it with the Biblical story of Jacob and Laban; ac-

Other types of magical power are attributed to Hermes in the oldest myths, in which he is trickster rather than thief. The gods selected Hermes to steal Ares out of the brazen pot not only because this had to be accomplished stealthily, but also because magical skill was needed. This myth belongs to the folk-tale type of the "demon caught in a bottle or other receptacle," a famous example of which is one of the Arabian Nights tales. In this type of story both the imprisonment and the release of the demon are magical exercises. Both Hermes' magical power to release and the attendant power to bind are further illustrated by the so-called cursing tablets which excavations have uncovered. These leaden tablets, which are inscribed with curses against persons named on them and then buried in the ground, were credited with maleficent power. The Greek word for these cursing tablets means "bindings," and a number of them invoke Hermes as "the one who holds down" or, as we say, "the spellbinder." Because of his power to bind and to release, Hermes was the god who prevented the souls of the dead from leaving the tomb, and who presided over the Greek All-Souls festival, the Anthesteria, when the ghosts of the dead returned for one night to partake of a meal set out for them by the living.[19]

Related to this same power of binding is the "skill at

---

tually Jacob secured Laban's cattle by magical trickery (*Genesis*, 30:37–39).

[19] The story of Ares in the brazen pot was compared to the general folktale type by Radermacher in his *Homerische Hermeshymnus*, 181. In medieval times legends of this kind gathered round the names of Paracelsus and Vergil; see Bolte-Polívka, *Anmerkungen zu den Kinder- und Hausmärchen der Brüder Grimm*, II, 414–422. On the cursing tablets (καταδέσεις), and Hermes κάτοχος, see Nilsson, *Greek Popular Religion*, 113–115 and F. B. Jevons, "Graeco-Italian Magic," in Marett, *Anthropology and the Classics*, 108–113. On the Anthesteria, see Farnell, *Cults*, V, 12, 219–221; Nilsson, *op. cit.*, p. 143, plate 2; and Deubner, *Attische Feste*, 93–122.

the oath" which Hermes bestowed upon Autolycus. An
oath is a curse, a magic formula that binds parties to a
given action. As the etymology of the Greek word
shows, it is something which restricts or ties; that
power lies in the words themselves, which are magical,
as are the words inscribed on the cursing tablets.
Hermes is the master of the magic formulae which
bind.[20]

In the myth of Pandora, Hermes' gift of "lies and
deceitful words and a stealthy disposition" is the gift of
guile in sexual seduction. Seduction was, throughout
Greek civilization, a magic art, employing love-charms,
compulsive magic directed at the person desired, and
supplicatory rituals invoking the deities of love—of
whom Hermes was one, and Aphrodite the foremost.
The interpenetration of the notions of trickery and
magic in the art of seduction is illustrated by Homer's
phrase "the beguiling words of love-making, which
trick the mind even of the wise": Homer is describing
the properties of Aphrodite's girdle, borrowed by Hera
as a love-charm to attract Zeus. Another illustration is
the epithet "weaver of tricks" applied to Aphrodite by
Sappho. A lover might invoke Aphrodite "weaver of
tricks" or Hermes the Trickster. In fact, Hermes and

[20] On the Greek concept of the oath, see Hirzel, "Der Eid als
Fluch," in *Der Eid*, 137–141, and Boisacq, *s.v.* ὅρκος; on the
Indo-European concept, see Schrader, *Reallexikon, s.v.* "Eid,"
I, 229; on the primitive concept, see Thurnwald in Ebert, *Reallexikon, s.v.* "Eid," III, 38–39. In the classical period of Greek
civilization the art of words was conceived more rationally, as
the art of rhetoric. Whereas Hermes was the master of words
throughout Greek culture, in the classical period this meant primarily that he was the god of rhetoric. See Eitrem, in Pauly-
Wissowa, VIII.782; the earliest instance is in the *Hymn*, 325–
396. But throughout the classical period the cursing
tablets show, the earlier concept of Hermes as the master of
word-magic persisted in the underworld of popular superstition,
to rise again, under the sign of Hermes Trismegistus, in the later
Hellenistic civilization, when popular superstitions became the
dominant religious force. See Kern, *Religion der Griechen*, II,
19.

Aphrodite were frequently associated in ritual, and even combined in the figure of Hermaphroditus. This association was undoubtedly due to the fact that both cults operated in the realm of love-magic.[21]

One epithet, "the whisperer," which was shared by Hermes, Aphrodite, and Eros, underlines the connection between Hermes the master of love-magic and Hermes the master of magic words. The epithet implies that a special virtue is attached to *whispered* words. It is a common enough principle of primitive magic that certain spells and incantations must be recited or crooned in a low voice, or whispered. The old Germanic *runes*—magic formulae of various sorts, including love-spells—are a good example of this custom; the word *rune*, we are told, "from the same root as the German *raunen* (to whisper), signifies, in the first instance, whispering, secret speech, and then mystery in general, in doctrine, witchcraft, song, symbol, or letter." In Theocritus' second *Idyll* a woman chants a spell to bring back her lover; it is expressly

---

[21] *Iliad*, 14.216–217 (ἔκλεψε); Sappho, Frg. 1 (δολόπλοκος). On the association of Hermes with Aphrodite, see Eitrem, in Pauly-Wissowa, VIII.760–761; Preller-Robert, I, 387–388; and Farnell, *Cults*, II, 742; V, 10–11. All these authorities explain the association on the ground that both were fertility cults. But, as we shall see later, there is no solid evidence that Hermes was a fertility god. In any case, in the specific rituals where Hermes and Aphrodite are linked, there is no unambiguous instance of fertility as the object (it is not clear what the object is in Pausanias, II.19.6 and VI.26.5, and Aristophanes, *Peace*, 456). On the other hand, when Eros (Love) or Peitho (Persuasion) is joined with Hermes and Aphrodite, or when Aphrodite bears the epithet "contriver" (μαχανῖτις), (Pausanias, VII.31.6), it is clear that the object is simply the winning of the beloved. This was the explanation given by the Greeks themselves: Plutarch (*Conjugalia Praecepta*, 138C) says that the reason why Hermes and Aphrodite were constantly associated in ancient Greek religion is that "words" and "Persuasion" are so important in love. Plutarch is thinking of Hermes the god of eloquence; to apply his thought to the primitive period, we must substitute for the concept of the god of eloquence the concept of the god of magic spells. See above, note 20.

stated that the magic words are "crooned softly."
Hermes the "whisperer" is Hermes the master of
runes.[22]

Hermes is not only the master of magic words; he
also has a magic wand. His most ancient and common-
est attribute was a rod, about the length of a man's
arm, surmounted by a convolution best described as a
figure eight, the upper circle of which was left open at
the top. In shape Hermes' rod bears a close resem-
blance to the magician's forked rod in German folk-

[22] For Hermes ψίθυρος, see Eitrem, in Pauly-Wissowa, VIII.
774; Roscher, *Lexikon der Mythologie, s.v.* "Psithyros," III,
3198–3199; Preller-Robert, Vol. I, p. 368, note 3. On the Germanic runes, see P. D. Chantepie de la Saussaye, *The Religion
of the Teutons* (Boston, 1902), 388; cf. the Latin *susurrus
magicus* (Justinian, *Institutions,* IV.18.5; Apuleius, *Metamorphoses,* I.3; and Ovid, *Metamorphoses,* XIV.57). On Theocritus,
Idylls, II.11 (ποταείσομαι ἄσυχα), see R. J. Cholmeley, *Theocritus* (London, 1930), 386–388. Cf. Aeschylus, *Supplices,* 1034–
1042, where Aphrodite "the whisperer" is invoked along with
"Persuasion, the magic charmer," and described as "goddess of
tricky counsel." In the Septuagint (*Ecclesiastes,* 10:11) the
incantation of a snake-charmer is termed "whispering." The root
sometimes has the meaning "slander," i.e., magically maleficent
words, as in the cursing tablets. Usener in his discussion of the
epithet adduces the custom of whispering prayers into the ear of
the image of the god, as well as the Hero called "Whisperer,"
whose shrine stood beside the temple of Athena at Lindos and
whose function was to mediate between humanity and the great
goddess by passing on to her, in a whisper, the prayers of her
suppliants. H. Usener, "Psithyros," *Rheinisches Museum,* 59
(1904):623–624. Usener, however, inferred that the epithet, as
applied to Hermes and Aphrodite, meant "whispered to," not
"whispering." This is philologically impossible (cf. Pindar, *Pythian,* II.75, and Aristophanes, Frg. 167, ed. Hall and Geldart).
Usener failed to see that the epithet was derived from a specific
magic practice. Its application to deity reflects the changes in
magic effected by the intrusion of a religion of personal gods.
Originally the whispered spell of the magician was sufficient to
accomplish the desired objective. Subsequently the Hero Whisperer takes over the magician's role; finally the magician's
power is wholly transferred to the gods. The evolution seems to
reflect a loss of self-confidence in man *vis-à-vis* the environment
he seeks to control; one may compare the evolution from the
naïve self-confidence of Homer's heroes to the insecurities, frus-
trations, and questionings of Hesiod.

lore; and it was made of gold, a substance frequently
credited with magical power, as in the golden bough
which was Aeneas' talisman on his journey through the
underworld.[23] In Greek myth and ritual the rod was
widely used as a magical instrument. It is with a touch
of the rod that the sorceress Circe transforms men into
swine. Because of its power to make dreams come true,
it became the symbol of a golden age of peace and
plenty. It was an indispensable instrument in commerce with the dead—the "ghost-drawing" rod. A ritual of the healing-god Asclepius was called "the lifting
up of the rod"; it was also carried in purificatory
processions to the crossroads. The Greeks placed representations of this rod at the entrance to their houses,
probably because of its purificatory value, or perhaps
because it was the symbol of prosperity and good fortune.[24] Hermes' rod is specifically stated to have magical power: in Homer it is always "the rod with which
he *charms* men's eyes to sleep." Hermes with a rod in
his hand, as he appears on Greek vases, is Hermes the
magician with his magic wand.[25]

[23] On the Greek rod ($\dot{\rho}\acute{\alpha}\beta\delta os$), see Boetzkes, in Pauly-Wissowa,
s.v. "Kerykeion," XI.331–341; Crome, "Kerykeia," *Mitteilungen
des deutschen archäologischen Instituts, Athenische Abteilung,*
63 (1938):117–126; *Iliad,* 24.343; *Odyssey,* 5.87; 10.277; 24.3;
Hymn, 530. On the German *Wünschelruth,* see J. Grimm,
Deutsche Mythologie (4th ed., Gütersloh, n.d.), II, 814–816;
Amira, *Der Stab in der germanischen Rechtsymbolik,* 11–12, 23,
162–163. On the magical power of gold, see E. Norden, *P.
Vergilius Maro Aeneis Buch VI* (2d ed., Berlin, 1916), 172.

[24] For the transforming power of the rod, see *Odyssey* 10.238,
319; 13.429; 16.172. For the rod as a symbol of plenty, see
Crome, *op. cit.,* 126; Norden *loc. cit.;* Arrian, *Epicteti Disserta-
tiones,* III.20.12. For the "ghost-drawing" rod, see Norden,
loc. cit.; cf. the vase in Reinach, *Répertoire des vases peints,*
II, 319. For the "lifting up of the rod," see Nilsson, *Griechische
Feste,* 411; Pauly-Wissowa, Part II, Vol. I, p. 18. For the proces-
sion to the crossroads, see Eustathius on *Odyssey,* 22.481. For
the rod at the entrance to houses, see Pauly-Wissowa, XI.338.

[25] *Iliad,* 24.343, etc. Hermes has the rod when he conducts
the dead suitors of Penelope to the underworld in *Odyssey*
24.1–4; the rod with which Hermes shepherds the ghosts is his

Thus Hermes was magician, and Hermes was trickster. But what is the relation between the two? By and large, the primitive mind makes no distinction between trickery and magic. Modern science would agree, but with this difference: for the scientist the belief in natural causation reduces magic to mere trickery; the primitive, referring the unintelligible to supernatural causes, regards all trickery as magic. The modern view is based on a clear distinction between the two, which is precisely what the primitive lacks.

The Greeks of the classical period, who cannot be called primitives, made a distinction between trickery and magic comparable to our own, just as they distinguished between trickery and theft. But this distinction did not exist at an earlier period of the Greek language. The words connoting magical action in the classical period are derived from roots whose original meaning is just as close to the notion of trickery as it is to that of magic.[26] This original ambiguity is preserved in archaic Greek; for example, the word φηλήτης, which is from the same root as θέλγειν, to "charm," is used in the *Hymn* with the connotation of "thief," to describe Hermes, and is used by Hesiod with the connotation of "trickster" to describe womankind—"he who puts his trust in woman, puts his trust in *tricksters*."[27] Conversely, the word δόλος, which in the

---

usual one (compare the epithet χρυσόρραπις with *Iliad*, 24.343); it is therefore erroneous to say that for conducting souls Hermes uses the smaller ferule depicted on the Jena vase (Harrison, *Prolegomena to the Study of Greek Religion*, 44–46; Boetzkes, in Pauly-Wissowa, XI.335). With his usual wand he attends ghost-scenes (ψυχοστασίαι); see Roscher, *Lexikon der Mythologie*, II, 1142, Abb. 2. With his usual wand he wards off "ghostly influences" (κῆρες); see *Hymn*, 530.

[26] See Boisacq, *s.v.* θέλγω (from the same root as the Latin *fallo*) and κηλέω (from the same root as the Latin *calvor, calumnia*).

[27] See above, notes 15 and 16. In view of the connotation of magic inherent in the root, and our previous analysis of sexual

classical period meant trickery, in archaic Greek carries implications of magic. If we accept the terms
"trick" and "tricky" as its equivalents in English, we
find that Homer characterizes the sorceresses Circe
and Calypso as "tricky"; the power of Proteus, the old
man of the sea, to turn himself into various animals is
described as a "tricky skill"; food that Circe may have
poisoned with a magic drug, the magic, unbreakable
chains that Hephaestus forged to catch Ares and
Aphrodite, a phantom created by a god to mislead
men—these are all called "tricks." In the story of the
phantom we find the combination, "Apollo charmed
(ἔθελγε) him with a trick." [28]

The root κλέπτειν, which, with the root δόλος, fur-
nishes the characteristic terms for Hermes the Trickster and, later, Hermes the Thief, throws further light
on the primitive concept of magic. Its original meaning was "secret action." To the primitive mind "secret
action" means magic. The connotation of magic in the
root κλέπτειν is apparent in the examples already considered: it is applied to the magic action of releasing
Ares, to Pandora's magic powers of seduction, to the
magic power of seduction in Aphrodite's girdle, and to
Autolycus' skill in the magic formulae of oaths. In the
Hymn the rope with which Apollo tries to lead away
his refound cattle magically takes root in the ground,
through the will of Hermes the "stealthy-minded"
(κγεψίφρονος), that is to say, the magician. [29]

---

seduction as magic, the word φηλήτης in the Hesiodic passage
must be interpreted as implying magical powers: Hesiod is
saying that women are *bewitching* tricksters.
    [28] *Odyssey,* 7.245; 9.32; 23.321; 4.455; 10.380; 8.276, 282,
317; *Iliad,* 21.599–604. Cf. *Homeric Hymn to Demeter,* 8.
    [29] *Hymn,* 413; cf. Aristotle, *Rhetoric,* 1408b.5; κλέπτεται ὁ
ἀκροατής, "the listener is held spellbound." For the view that
magic is essentially action regarded as mysterious and occult in
character, see E. Westermarck, *Ritual and Belief in Morocco*
(London, 1926), I, 21, and B. Malinowski, *Argonauts of the*

Not only Hermes but also the great Zeus himself was called "stealthy." In the light of our analysis of the word, this is not at all surprising; anyone who has read A. B. Cook's monumental study of Zeus will recognize the propriety of calling Zeus "Him of the magic powers." None of the scholars who interpret Hermes the "stealthy" as Hermes the Thief has, so far as I know, given any explanation of why Zeus should be called "thievish." [30]

Thus an analysis of the oldest stratum of Greek mythology reveals that behind Hermes the Thief is Hermes the Trickster, and behind Hermes the Trickster is Hermes the Magician. This approach to a large extent disposes of the question why trickery should have a divine patron. In the Golden Bough we read:

A vestige of the transition from magic to religion may perhaps be discerned in the belief, shared by many peoples, that the gods themselves are adepts in magic, guarding their persons by talismans and working their wills by spells and incantations. . . . In Babylonia the great god Ea was reputed to be the inventor of magic, and his son Marduk, the chief deity of Babylon, inherited the art from his father. Marduk is described as "the master of exorcism, the magician of the gods." Another text declares that "the incantation is the incantation of Marduk, the exorcist is the image of Marduk." . . . In the Vedic religion the gods are often represented as attaining their ends by magical means; in particular the god Brhaspati, "the creator of prayers," is

---

Western Pacific (London, 1922), 420. Another illustration is the Greek verb for "hide," κρύπτω: in Euripides, Andromache, 32, "hidden drugs" means magic drugs; in Iliad, 14.168, the magic lock made by Hephaestus for Zeus's bedroom is called a "hidden lock." For the same reason Hermes the "Whisperer" is very nearly identical with Hermes the Magician: whispered (i.e., secretly recited) words are to magic words as secret action is to magic action. Cf. Aeschylus, Supplices, 1034–1042, and note 22 above.

[30] Hesychius, s.v. ἐπικλόπιος. Zeus the "stealthy" is akin to the "crooked-counselled" Zeus of Homer.

regarded as "the heavenly embodiment of the priesthood, in so far as the priesthood is invested with the power, and charged with the task, of influencing the course of things by prayers and spells"; in short, he is "the possessor of the magical power of the holy word." So too in Norse mythology Odin is said to have owed his supremacy and his dominion over nature to his knowledge of the runes or magical names of all things in earth and heaven. . . . In short, many gods may at first have been merely deified sorcerers.[31]

With this somewhat fuller understanding of Hermes the Thief we can connect this one of the god's several roles with another which superficially seems wholly unrelated—Hermes the Craftsman. The relation between primitive craftsmanship and magic, although difficult to define, is admittedly close. Primitive magic is a technology of a sort; its aim is the manipulation of the external world. The primitive craftsman supplements his technique with magical practices, and success at his craft is taken to indicate possession of magical powers.[32]

Hermes the Craftsman is celebrated in myths of various types. In some he is described as an inventor: in the *Homeric Hymn* the lyre, the rustic pipe, and the art of making fire with firesticks are all said to be his discoveries. In others he is recognized as the patron god of specific crafts, notably those of the shepherd and the herald. In Attic drama, and even in Homer, he often plays the role of the divine servant, the heavenly counterpart of the menial laborer as a social class: in the *Odyssey* a journeyman is said to owe his profi-

[31] J. G. Frazer, *The Magic Art*, I, 240–242.
[32] On craft-magic among the Indo-European peoples, see O. Schrader, *Sprachvergleichung und Urgeschichte*, II, 20–28; on craft-magic in Greek religion, see Gernet and Boulanger, *Génie grec dans la religion*, 78–81. The Greeks attributed the discovery of iron-smelting to magicians (the Idaean Dactyls); see Phoronis, quoted by the scholiast on Apollonius Rhodius, *Argonautica*, I.1126–1131 (*Epicorum Graecorum Fragmenta*, ed. G. Kinkel, I, 211).

ciency to Hermes, who "bestows joy and glory on the
works of all mankind." As a craftsman-god, Hermes is
endowed with the essential traits of the mythological
type of culture hero, of which there is no finer example
than the Greek Prometheus. Like Prometheus, Hermes
is represented as "pre-eminently intelligent": the primitive mind knows not our antithesis of mental and
manual labor and regards craftsmanship and mental
ability as going hand in hand. Like Prometheus again,
Hermes is represented as a friend of mankind, a source
of material blessings, "the giver of good things," "the
giver of joy." [33]

The connection between Hermes the Magician and
Hermes the Craftsman is best shown by a semantic
study of the same key words in the cult of Hermes
which elucidate the relation between theft and trickery, and between trickery and magic. The word δόλος,
"trick," which in Homeric Greek has connotations of
magical action, is also used interchangeably with the
usual word for "technical skill" (τέχνη) to denote
Hephaestus' magic skill at craftsmanship as well as the
products of that skill. The root κλέπτειν, "steal," which
in Homeric Greek has connotations of magical trick-

[33] For Hermes the inventor, see *Hymn*, 25, 111, 511; cf.
Diodorus, V.75; scholiast on *Odyssey*, 16.471; Farnell, *Cults*,
Vol. V, p. 62, ref. 2; and Horace, *Odes*, I.10. Hermes is also a
patron of the medical art; see *Odyssey*, 10.302–306, and Eitrem
in Pauly-Wissowa, VIII.788. For Hermes the divine servant, see
Odyssey, 15.319–324; Aeschylus, *Prometheus Vinctus*, 941–942;
Euripides, *Ion*, 4; Aristophanes, *Peace*, 201, 429; and *Plutus*,
1170. For Hermes the preeminently intelligent, see *Iliad*, 20.35,
and Boisacq, *s.v.* ἐριούνιος, ἀκάκητα. For Hermes the giver of
good things (δῶτορ' ἐάων), see *Odyssey*, 8.335. For Hermes the
giver of joy (χαριδότης), see Plutarch, *Greek Questions*, 55.
These last two epithets are usually interpreted as referring to
gifts of agricultural produce, on the hypothesis that Hermes was
a fertility god. This hypothesis, we shall see, is unsubstantiated.
In the passage in the *Odyssey* (15.320) where Hermes is said
to bestow *joy* on human works the reference is to the products of
craftsmanship. Hephaestus' wife was also called Χάρις; see *Iliad*,
18.382.

ery, is also used to denote technical proficiency: if "stealthy" is taken as the English equivalent of the word ἐπίκλοπος (the same word used to describe the *stealthy* disposition Hermes gave to Pandora), we find Homer saying "a smooth talker and *stealthy* in the use of words," and "*stealthy* in the use of the bow." The latter passage shows that the aptness of the root as applied to technical skill derives from its basic meaning of "secret, mysterious action": Odysseus' skill with the bow is *uncanny*.[34]

In the modern view, technical proficiency excludes trickery: that is to say, we regard cheating as the antithesis of good workmanship. Hence modern scholars have felt obliged to brand the cult of Hermes the "tricky" as immoral. The Greeks themselves, in the postclassical period, felt the same way: Pausanias, the Greek antiquarian of the second century A.D., says: "though Hermes is called the tricky, he stands ready to fulfil the prayers of men." In other words, Hermes' name is "the tricky," but his function is to promote human welfare, the function implied by the epithets "giver of good" and "giver of joy." To Pausanias the two aspects of Hermes' nature are contradictory, but they were not so to the Greeks of the Homeric age.

The Homeric concept is illustrated by the semantics of another important word in the cult of Hermes, κέρδος. In the classical period the noun κέρδος was the regular word for economic gain or profit, the pursuit of which was under the patronage of Hermes, and the adjective κερδῷος was one of the standard epithets applied to Hermes, with the meaning "gainful," "good at securing profit." In Homeric usage, however, the meaning of words of this root oscillates between "gain," "trickery," and "skill." The basic meaning of

[34] For δόλος see *Odyssey*, 4.455; 8.276, 282, 297, 317, 327, 332. For ἐπίκλοπος see *Iliad*, 22.281, and *Odyssey*, 21.397; cf. the story in Herodotus, IV, 9–10.

the root is "skill at making or doing things"; it is related to the Sanskrit *krtya*, meaning "a doing," especially a magic practice, and to the Irish *cerd*, meaning
a "craft" or "craftsman," with special reference to the
craft of the smith and of the poet. In this root the combination of "trickery" and "technical skill" is joined
by a third notion, that of the "gain" which results
from "trickery" or skill. This "gain" is essentially the
same as the "good" which Hermes gives. Once it is
seen that to the primitive Greeks "trickery" meant only
mysterious, magical action, it becomes clear why Hermes the "tricky" should "stand ready to fulfil the
prayers of men." Hermes the Trickster is identical
with Hermes the "giver of good things," the culture
hero. The interpenetration of these two aspects of
Hermes' mythological personality is perfectly illustrated in a description of the god in early Greek
poetry: "The Father called him the Clever One
(ἐριούνιον) because he excelled all the blessed gods and
mortal men in gainful crafts (κέρδεσι) and stealthy
skills (κλεπτοσύναις τεχνηέσσαις)." [35]

This combination of trickster and culture hero is a
recurrent phenomenon in primitive mythologies. In
Greek mythology there is one other well-known example—Prometheus, who is (1) a patron of handi-
crafts and a benefactor of mankind, (2) a cunning
trickster, and (3) a thief, as in the story of how he stole
fire from heaven to give it to men. Loki, in Eddic mythology, is a famous trickster; the most recent study
emphasizes that he is also a culture hero. In the my-

[35] For the cult of Hermes the "tricky" (δόλιος), see Pausanias,
VII.27.1; it is called "immoral" by Farnell (*Cults*, V. 23).
For the connection between Hermes and κέρδος, see the passage
from the Phoronis (translated above) in *Etymologicum Mag-
num*, 374.23; *Hymn*, 162, 260, 463; and Plutarch, *De Tranquil-
litate Animi*, 472B. On the meaning of the root κέρδος, see
Ebeling and Boisacq, *s.v.* κέρδος; Walde, *Vergleichendes Wörterbuch der indogermanischen Sprache*, I, 423; and Schrader, *Reallexikon*, II, 675.

thology of the North American Indians there is a recurrent figure that appears in the mixed role of altruistic
culture hero, shaman, and trickster. One example, the
Coyote, has been thus described: "In a multitude of
stories he is represented as contemptible—deceitful,
greedy, bestial, with an erotic mania that leads him to
incest, often outwitted by the animals whom he en-
deavours to trick, without gratitude to those that help
him; and yet, with all this, he is shown as a mighty
magician, reducing the world to order and helping
man with innumerable benefactions." In an interesting
variation, found in North America and Australia, the
two aspects are dissociated and projected into a pair of
brothers, one of whom is wise and benevolent, the
other mischievous and foolish, just as Prometheus and
his brother Epimetheus are represented in Greek mythology. Another famous example of the mischievous
trickster is the serpent, "who was more subtil than any
beast of the field," and who tempted Eve to eat of the
fruit of the tree of knowledge. In the parallel myth of
Pandora, Hermes, whom we may call more "subtil"
than any god in heaven, plays the same role: he does
not tempt Pandora, but he is responsible for her
"stealthy disposition," and thus for the fateful dénoue-
ment.[36]

[36] The identity of the trickster with the culture hero has been
clearly stated by three Dutch scholars; Kristensen, "De goddelijke bedrieger," *Mededeelingen der koninklijke Akademie van
wetenschappen, Amsterdam, Afdeeling Letterkunde,* Deel. 63,
Serie B (1927–28): 63–88; de Josselin de Jong, "De oorsprong
van den goddelijken bedrieger," *ibid.,* Deel. 68, Serie B (1929):
1–30; and de Vries, *The Problem of Loki.* On the culture hero of
the North American Indians, see A. van Deursen, *Der Heilbringer, eine ethnologische Studie über den Heilbringer bei
den nordamerikanischen Indianern* (Groningen, 1931). On the
Coyote, see H. B. Alexander, *North American Mythology* (*The
Mythology of All Races,* edited by L. H. Gray, Vol. X, Boston,
1916), 142. Like the Coyote, Hermes is the hero of a large number of erotic adventures; (see Eitrem, in Pauly-Wissowa, VIII.
774); cf. the connection between Hermes and love-magic discussed above. On the Australian examples, see R. H. Codring-

If Hermes is one of those gods who are described in
the *Golden Bough* as merely deified sorcerers, can we
name his earthly counterpart? Of all the professions
patronized by Hermes, the one most closely identified
with the god is that of the herald. In the Homeric
Pantheon Hermes is the herald of the gods; conversely,
the earthly herald is always regarded as a peculiar son
of Hermes. We think of the herald as a sort of town-
crier—a job requiring little skill, with nothing mysterious, magical, or "tricksterish" about it. Superficially the
work of the Homeric heralds is equally prosaic. They
belong to the staff of the king, whom they assist in
the execution of his administrative duties by calling
the people to assembly, keeping order at the assembly,
and going on embassies; in this respect they are comparable to the beadle attached to certain English mag-
istrates. They also render the king personal service,
particularly at royal banquets, where they even have
the menial duty of washing the tables; they prepare
the royal bath. There is, however, another side to
the picture. The heralds are called "public workers"
($\delta\eta\mu\iota o\epsilon\rho\gamma o\iota$), a term which is applied also to seers,
healers, woodworkers, and bards, and which connotes
a socially useful and respected craft. The special
knowledge they possess is emphasized in a series of
stock epithets meaning "wise," or "knowing." It is a
highly paid craft: we hear of a herald "rich in gold
and bronze." More than that, it is a sacred craft: heralds are "dear to Zeus," "the messengers of Zeus and
of men"; their persons are sacred and inviolate. They
are functionaries in sacred ceremonies, such as sacrifices and the ritual of divination by lottery; even the
royal banquets at which they minister are in essence
sacred meals. The herald's badge of office is a staff,

---

ton, *The Melanesians* (Oxford, 1891), 155–169. On Prometheus
and Epimetheus, see Hesiod, *Theogony*, 510–513, and *Works
and Days*, 85–89; Plato, *Protagoras*, 320D–321C.

which is respected as magically potent: oaths are taken
on it; it imposes an armistice on fighting warriors
when placed between them; in the hands of judges
"sitting in the sacred circle" it gives binding force to
their judgments; with the staff the proceedings of the
assembly are regulated.[37]

The interesting thing about the Homeric herald is
the diversity of functions combined in his office. In his
personal service to the king he sometimes seems no
more than a cook; yet he is the sacrosanct agent of international negotiations, in which capacity he resem-
bles the priests of that exalted Roman college the *fe-
tiales*. There can be no doubt that the primary function
of the herald is his ceremonial ministry, and that his
craft is the all-important one of knowing certain ceremonial proprieties. The Homeric priest is a functionary
attached to a temple; Homeric religion is not, as later
Greek religion was, organized primarily around
temples. The herald is the ceremonial expert in the rituals that center around the royal palace, the public assembly place, and the like. His "town-crying" function
is derived from his ceremonial function: political institutions at this rudimentary stage needed the support of
religious sanctions, and were organized as religious
ceremonies; hence a role was allotted to the ceremonial
expert, the herald. This political role, however, was
secondary: the suitors of the *Odyssey* needed the ceremonial ministry of a herald in their siege at Odysseus'
palace, although there had been no public assembly in
Ithaca for twenty years; the Attic clan of the "Heralds," who claimed descent from Hermes, were minis-
ters in the Eleusinian mysteries, not town-criers. Similarly, the personal service which the herald rendered
the king was a by-product of his ceremonial functions.
In Homeric society public religion was the responsibil-

[37] Buchholz, *Homerischen Realien*, II, 49–58; Wilamowitz,
Aristoteles und Athen, I, 202; Laum, *Heiliges Geld*, 45–56.

ity of the king, with the result that the ceremonial expert became an acolyte to the king. The king presides over the assembly, the heralds keep order; the king makes a sacrifice, the herald prepares the sacrificial animal; the king has a ceremonial banquet, the herald takes care of such ceremonial niceties as the proper division of the meat into portions. This ceremonial function is naturally extended to include the purely secular services which the king expects from all his attendants.

The ceremonial art of the herald has obvious affinities with the magic art of Hermes. The herald's magic staff has the same symbolic significance as Hermes' magic wand, despite the difference in shape. In recognition of the functional equivalence of the two, the difference in shape was later abolished: beginning in the late archaic period and continuing through the classical period, the herald carried a wand just like Hermes', and Hermes' wand came to be known as "the herald's thing." Whatever may be the explanation for the earlier difference in shape, the magic wand must have been attributed to Hermes in imitation of the similar instrument wielded by the herald.[38]

While the affinity between Hermes' magic art and the herald's ceremonial art is close, there is an unmistakable divergence between the many-sided magical activities of Hermes in the world of myth and the restricted role of the Homeric herald. The difference lies less in the nature of the skill they exercise than in the

[38] Boetzkes, in Pauly-Wissowa, s.v. "Kerykeion," XI.331; Crome, "Kerykeia," op. cit., 117–126; Harrison, Prolegomena to the Study of Greek Religion, 44–46. Both Crome and Harrison fail to appreciate the magical aspect of the herald's craft and hence the magical significance of his staff. Besides the herald (and of course the king), the priest, the necromancer, the prophetess, and the bard carried the staff as their badge; see Iliad, 1.15; Odyssey, 11.91; Hesiod, Theogony, 30; and Aeschylus, Agamemnon, 1265. See also Amira, Der Stab in der germanischen Rechtsymbolik, 11–12, 23, 123, 162; Gruppe, Griechische Mythologie und Religionsgeschichte, Vol. II, p. 896, note 3.

end to which their skills are directed. The myths of Hermes celebrate magic as a power to control nature, allied with craftsmanship, a source of material goods; the activities of the Homeric herald are strictly subordinated to the needs of Homeric kingship and hence, in the last analysis, are directed toward establishing and maintaining social control over men.

The distinction between magic directed toward the control of nature and magic allied with political power and directed toward the control of men is a by-product of the evolution of primitive society. Political domination is a relatively late innovation in human history; the magic art is older. Before it became allied with political power, magic was a peculiar form of primitive man's efforts to control his environment, as well as an expression of the feebleness of those efforts. When rulers or a ruling class emerged, they converted many of the traditions of the magic art into religious sanctions to bolster their own authority.

The discrepancy between Hermes the Magician and the Homeric herald may be explained on the hypothesis that the mythology records the role of the "herald" or magician before Homeric kingship existed, and that in Homer we see that role transformed as a result of the herald's subordination to the king. Archaeology dates the institution of kingship on the mainland of Greece to the period when the Mycenaean palaces were built (c. 1500–1200 B.C.), and identifies the civilization described in Homer with the Mycenaean period. Before this Homeric-Mycenaean age Greek culture was on a distinctly more primitive level. Remote as the pre-Homeric period is, it is the starting point for the evolution of the Greeks: in it lie the origins of later Greek institutions; from it is derived a substrate of primitive traditions in Greek mythology.[39]

---

[39] Nilsson, *Mycenaean Origin of Greek Mythology*, 221–251, and *Homer and Mycenae*, 266–272.

One of the few instruments we have for probing into
the pre-Homeric origins of Greek institutions is the
method of philological analysis which helped us grasp
the original significance of "tricksterishness." By trac-
ing the history of concepts back to their Indo-
European roots, modes of thought and behavior can be
uncovered which are obsolete in Homer. Such philological analysis reveals that the herald once had larger
scope for his ceremonial art than is allotted to him in
Homeric society. The etymological meaning of the
Greek word for "herald," κῆρυξ, is "expert sound-
maker." There is a corresponding emphasis on excellence of voice in a series of Homeric epithets applied to
heralds. It has always been taken for granted that this
attribute is ascribed to the herald because of his function of calling the assembly together. This assumption
would be plausible if town-crying were the original or
the basic function of the herald. The word for herald,
however, must have some connection with his ceremonial function; his ceremonial art must once have had
some connection with "sound-making." But what does
ceremonial "sound-making" mean? The etymology
suggests that the pre-Homeric herald had a functional
affinity with the singer or bard. The Greek word for
"herald" is related to the Latin carmen, a "song," and
the Sanskrit karuh, to "sing," and karus, a "bard." Some
of the Homeric epithets signifying "excellence of voice"
are applied by Homer to both heralds and bards.[40]

In the Indo-European languages words meaning
"song," as well as words meaning "speech," are commonly derived from roots meaning "loud sound"; the
root from which κῆρυξ and carmen are derived is only
one instance of a widespread phenomenon. Furthermore, these roots commonly have connotations of
magic. Philologists have therefore concluded that the

[40] Boisacq, s.v. κῆρυξ; Buchholz, Homerischen Realien, II,
56–57.

origins of song and poetry lie in the intoned formulae
of magical incantations. Anthropologists, who reach
the same conclusion on the basis of different evidence,
say that primitive magic has three essential ingredients: certain words spoken or chanted, certain ceremonial actions, and an officiating minister of the ceremony. The officiating minister leads both the "things
done" and the "things said [or sung]"—to borrow a
terminology used by the Greeks themselves in discuss-
ing the ritual origins of Greek tragedy; he is both the
leader in song and the leader in ceremony; in other
words, he is both "herald" and bard. By the time of
Homer, ritual exists without song, and song without
ritual, and each has its own expert. Thus the two
crafts of the herald and the bard seem to have been
derived from the single craft of the leader in magic
ritual.[41]

The craft of the pre-Homeric "herald," the leader in
both the rituals and the incantations of primitive
magic, inspired the mythological concept of the deity
who is himself both a herald and a magician. Hermes
is not the only figure in Greek mythology who combines these two functions: Prometheus not only shares
with Hermes the roles of thief, trickster, and culture
hero but is also a ceremonial expert and specifically a
herald. Hence the mythology of the trickster-god is
itself additional evidence of the activities of the pre-
Homeric "herald"; he must have been, like Hermes, expert in runes and other forms of word-magic, in love-

[41] See "Dichtkunst" and "Zauber" in Schrader, *Reallexikon;*
Jevons, "Graeco-Italian Magic," *op. cit.,* 96; Boisacq, *s.v.* εἴρω;
γόης; βασκαίνω; Malinowski, *Myth in Primitive Psychology,* 82–
83; W. S. Teuffel, *Geschichte der römischen Literatur* (6th ed.,
revised by W. Kroll and F. Skutch, Leipzig, 1916), I, 123. The
ritual origin of the craft of the bard explains why throughout
classical antiquity it was regarded as a sacred, magical craft. The
affinity between bard and herald is further indicated by the fact
that both carry the magic staff as their badge. See note 38
above.

magic, and in work-magic. Further light is thrown on these institutions by analysis of the other aspect of the cult of Hermes—the rituals, which are the subject of the next chapter.[42]

[42] On Prometheus as herald, see Hesychius, *s.v.* 'Ιθάς; Preller-Robert, I, 94–95. Aeschylus, in *Prometheus Vinctus* (line 461), makes Prometheus claim to have taught mankind "the Memory of all things, the Mother of the Muses and helpmate of workmen"; his thought seems to be that the culture hero must also have been the founder of the art of song; the magic art of the primitive "herald" combined both these functions.

CHAPTER

2

TRIBAL CUSTOMS

The cult of Hermes, like the cults of the other Greek gods, comprises not only a complex of myths but also a complex of rituals, which contain an original core corresponding to the original core of the mythology. In the cult of Hermes the basic rituals revolve around two objects—the sacred stone-heap and the sacred phallus. The name Hermes is probably derived from the Greek word for "stone-heap," ἕρμα, and signifies "he of the stone-heap." Representations of Hermes in classical times usually took the form of a square-cut ithyphallic block of stone surmounted with the god's head; this art-type was called a "herm" because, although occasionally extended to other gods, it was originally a distinctive characteristic of the cult of Hermes. What is the connection between Hermes the ithyphallic god of the stone-heap and Hermes the trickster and culture hero? [1]

[1] Preller-Robert, I, 401; Farnell, *Cults,* V, 7; Eitrem, in Pauly-

The stone-heaps were a primitive sort of boundary-stone, marking a point of communication between strangers. They were placed at the entrance of a house, where visitors were received; at crossroads or some other point on a road where strangers met habitually; in a forest or on some hilltop, both of which in a land like Greece constitute natural boundaries. In primitive Greece, as in other cultures where the basic unit of society is not the individual but the family or clan, religious and social institutions were strongly affected by distrust of the stranger, the member of an alien family group. Intercourse with strangers was surrounded with magical safeguards: meetings occasioned magico-religious ceremonies; points of habitual contact were regarded as hallowed ground; natural or artificial boundaries, where the friendly world of one's own kindred ended and the inhospitable world of strangers began, could not be safely passed without the aid of ritual. The magic practices surrounding intercourse with strangers were naturally associated with the god of the boundary-stone. Even in classical times, when fear of the stranger had lost most of its force, honors were still rendered to Hermes as the "god of roads," the "god of doors," the "guide" who presides over all comings-in and goings-out, the "ambassador" who protects men in their dealings with strangers.[2]

Wissowa, VIII.738; Nilsson, *Griechische Feste*, 388, and *History of Greek Religion*, 109–110; Wilamowitz, *Glaube der Hellenen*, I, 159.

[2] On the stone-heaps and on Hermes the god of communication, see Farnell, *Cults*, V, 66–67; *Odyssey*, 16.471 and scholia; Aeschylus, *Agamemnon*, 283, and *Supplices*, 920; Sophocles, *Philoctetes*, 1459; Plato, *Laws*, 941A; and Pausanias, VIII.36.10. For the interpretation, see Farnell, *Cults*, V, 18; Wilamowitz, *Glaube der Hellenen*, I, 159; Nilsson, *Greek Popular Religion*, 8, 79; and Crome, "Hipparcheioi Hermai," *Mitteilungen des deutschen archäologischen Instituts, Athenische Abteilung*, 60–61 (1935–36): 312. On primitive boundaries see J. A. MacCulloch in Hastings' *Encyclopedia of Religion and Ethics*, *s.v.*

The magic art of dealing with strangers is well calculated to inspire the concept of the trickster-magician;
the stranger represents a hostile force which must be
outmaneuvered or tricked. Spellbinding, oath-making,
sexual seduction, and other forms of trickery reported
in the myths of Hermes are in fact various manifesta-
tions of his magic power to control strangers. Other
examples of the divine trickster have a similar connection with the magic practices regulating communication with strangers; for example, a recent study of the
trickster in the mythologies of the North American Indians and the Australian aborigines shows that the
concept is rooted in the rituals prescribed for ceremonial contacts between tribes.[3]

The meaning of the other sacred object in the cult of
Hermes, the phallus, is a controversial question. Most
scholars have assumed that it is a symbol of fertility, as
it undoubtedly is in the cults of Demeter and Dionysus. But this interpretation is open to fatal objections.
Unlike Demeter and Dionysus, Hermes was never regarded as a source of vegetable fertility, and the use of
the phallus as a symbol of fertility is inseparable from
vegetation magic, being derived from the notion that
ritual performance of the sexual act stimulates agricultural growth. Phallic symbols of the cult of Hermes
were placed on mountaintops, rural waysides, state
boundaries, city streets, in the doorways and court-
yards of houses, in gymnasia and libraries, in sacred

"Landmarks," VII, 792; H. S. Maine, Village Communities in
the East and West, 192–193; and Schrader, Reallexikon, s.v.
"Grenze," I, 410–411. On the social and religious implications
of the distrust of strangers, see Glotz, Solidarité de la famille,
Bk. I, Ch. 1, and pp. 138–140, 193–197; O. Schrader, Sprachvergleichung und Urgeschichte, II, 294; Frazer, Taboo and the
Perils of the Soul, 101–116.
[3] De Josselin de Jong, "De oorsprong van den goddelijken
bedrieger," Mededeelingen der koninklijke Akademie van wetenschappen, Amsterdam, Afdeeling Letterkunde, Deel. 68, Serie B
(1929):10–12, 18–20, 25–27.

precincts, and on graves; which of these is an appropriate place for a fertility symbol? The phallus in the
cult of Hermes is in fact found in much the same loca-
tions as the stone-heap, with which it was often combined. The two are equivalent symbols, and no one has
claimed that the stone-heap was ever a fertility symbol.[4]

To assume that the phallus is always a fertility symbol is to ignore its widespread use by various peoples,
including the Greeks and Romans, as an apotropaic
amulet, to bring good luck and avert evil. As such it
was very appropriately attached to Hermes, the magician and god of the boundary-stone. What more ap-

[4] The phallus in the cult of Hermes is interpreted as a fertility
symbol by Preller-Robert (I, 387–388), Farnell (*Cults*, V, 11–
12), Eitrem (Pauly-Wissowa, *s.v.* "Hermes," VIII.774–776),
and Goldman ("The Origin of the Greek Herm," *American
Journal of Archaeology*, 46 (1942):58–68). Farnell admits that
Hermes has nothing to do with vegetable fertility. The few
connections with vegetation listed by Eitrem can easily be explained as derivations from the apotropaic function of the herm
guarding the fields. See *Epigrammata Graeca* (ed. Kaibel), 812;
cf. Nilsson, *Griechische Feste*, 101. On the location of the ithyphallic herms see Eitrem, in Pauly-Wissowa, *s.v.* "Hermai,"
VIII.700–702, and Pausanias, VI.26.5. On their relation to the
stone-heaps, see Eitrem, *op. cit.*, VIII.697–698, and Herter, in
Pauly-Wissowa, *s.v.* "Phallos," XIX.1689–1690. The other arguments which have been advanced for classifying Hermes as a
fertility god are very inconclusive: 1. "Hermes was regarded as
potent to promote animal fertility"; this attribute may have been
derived from either his pastoral function (see Nilsson, *Griechische Feste*, 391–392) or his general magical powers (see
Hesiod, *Theogony*, 444). 2. "Hermes is connected with human
love and marriage"; but his function is to aid the lover in securing possession of the beloved, an end which is distinct from that
of procreation and which may be an end in itself (see above,
p. 15, and below, p. 44). 3. "Hermes is often associated with
Pan and the Nymphs, and these are vegetation deities"; but it is
equally plausible to suppose that the link between these deities
is their common habitat, the wild wasteland. 4. "Hermes is one
of the chthonic or 'earthy' divinities, such as Demeter, which
combine the powers of death and life"; but as a chthonic divinity Hermes' role is that of controlling communication between
the upper and nether worlds, as "conductor of souls." (See
Diogenes Laertius, VIII.31.)

propriate place for an apotropaic amulet than the
boundary separating the familiar *mine* from the inhospitable *not-mine?* The boundary-stones of the Romans
were frequently phallic in shape, and the ithyphallic
Priapus who guarded so many Roman gardens is described by Horace as "quelling thieves with his right
hand and with the crimson stick stretching from his
obscene groin." The phallus is so closely identified with
magic in Roman religion that the word *fascinum,*
meaning "enchantment," "witchcraft" (cf. "fascinate"),
is one of the standard Latin terms for the phallus; no
better evidence could be found for the appropriateness
of the emblem for Hermes as magician. When Greek
craftsmen hung images of ithyphallic demons over
their workshops, it is clear that to them the phallus
symbolized not fertility but magic skill at craftsmanship.[5]

[5] On the phallus as an amulet, see Hartland, in Hastings' *Encyclopedia of Religion and Ethics, s.v.* "Phallism," Vol. IX, especially pp. 818, 825–826, 829; Herter, in Pauly-Wissowa, *s.v.*
"Phallos," Vol. XIX, especially pp. 1733–1744; Sudhoff, in
Ebert's *Reallexikon, s.v.* "Amulett," I, 158; R. Briffault, *The
Mothers,* III, 201–202, 303–305; Nilsson, *Griechische Feste,* 102,
391; Kuhnert, in Pauly-Wissowa, *s.v.* "Fascinum," VI.2011–
2012; and Horace, *Satires,* I.8.3–5. On the ithyphallic demons,
see Herter, *op. cit.,* XIX.1695; cf. the ithyphallism attributed to
Hephaestus, the Cyclops, and the Idaean Dactyls (Pauly-
Wissowa, VIII.358; XI.2343; XIX.1687). Herter (*ibid.,* 1683–
1684) holds that the apotropaic function of the phallus is derived from its fertility-promoting function; his major premise is
that "by its very nature the phallus is a source of fertility." This
proposition may seem obvious to us; but would it be so obvious, for example, to those savages whom Malinowski (*Sexual
Life of Savages,* 153) could not persuade of the facts of physio-
logical paternity? Furthermore, the concept of the phallus as a
fertility symbol presupposes the existence of rituals of sexual
intercourse practiced to make crops grow; these practices in turn
presuppose a body of biological theory that could have been acquired only through the development of agriculture beyond the
rudimentary stages. In view of the relative recency, in human
history, of the development of agriculture, and the much greater
antiquity of the concept of the sexual act as precipitating magical influences, and of the phallus as a magical symbol, the truth
would appear to be just the opposite of Herter's contention. In

Hermes, the god of the boundary-stone, with his stone-heap and phallus, was revered not only as a magician who defended his people against the aggressions of strangers, but also as a culture hero. Through contact with strangers and strange places the primitive community supplemented its own limited resources with goods from beyond its boundaries. The boundary was crossed not only by goods secured through trade or barter with the strangers living "on the other side," but also by enterprising men bent on procuring raw materials from the wasteland that lay between neighboring communities, or engaged on a "merchant adventure" into alien territory. "Crossing the boundary" was, in the eyes of the primitive Greeks, the essence of trade and economic enterprise: the standard Greek words for "buy" and "do business" are derived from a root meaning "beyond, across." Thus Hermes the god of the boundary-stone became the god of trade and craftsmanship, and, consequently, a culture hero and "giver of good things." Close parallels are the two Roman gods of the boundary, Janus and Silvanus. Silvanus, who, like Hermes, presided over both the boundary and the adjoining wild wasteland, became the patron of the craftsmen who worked in the upland forests (*saltuarii*), such as quarry-workers and shepherds, and also of the traders who cross the boundary in the pursuit of gain. Janus, like Hermes, is a trickster and carries a magic wand; he was said to be the protector of enterprise of all sorts, and the inventor of various arts, including religious ritual; in an ancient Roman hymn he is called "good creator"—the Latin equivalent of "culture hero." [6]

---

the history of the phallus as a magical symbol, its application to vegetation magic is a late development.

[6] See Schrader, *Sprachvergleichung und Urgeschichte*, II, 297; Boisacq, *s.v.* πέρνημι, πιπράσκω, πράσσω (all from the root of πέραν); Klotz, in Pauly-Wissowa, Part II, Vol. III, *s.v.* "Sil-

The connection between Hermes the god of trade
and Hermes the god of the boundary-stone presupposes that, originally at least, commercial contacts took
place on the boundary. In classical times trade was
conducted in the agora, an open space in the center of
the city where the visiting merchant set up his shop.
But the use of the agora as a market-place does not
begin until the eighth century B.C.; the word agora
means literally "gathering-place," and in Homer it is
used only as a place of political and religious assembly.
The city market-place presupposes the city-state;
where did commercial contact take place in the earlier
period of village communities and autonomous clans?
In his classic study of the village community Sir Henry
Maine writes:

> In order to understand what a market originally was, you
> must try to picture to yourselves a territory occupied by
> village-communities, self-acting and as yet autonomous,
> each cultivating its arable land in the middle of its waste,
> and each, I fear I must add, at perpetual war with its neigh-
> bour. But at several points, points probably where the do-
> mains of two or three villages converged, there appear to
> have been spaces of what we should now call neutral
> ground. These were the Markets. They were probably the
> only places at which the members of the different primitive
> groups met for any purpose except warfare.[7]

In Greece the tradition of holding intercommunity
gatherings on the boundary survived the establishment

---

vanus"; W. F. Otto, in Pauly-Wissowa, Suppl. 3, s.v. "Janus."
Janus is called "good creator" in the Carmen Saliare; see Otto,
op. cit., 1176. On Janus as protector of enterprise, see Roscher,
Lexikon der Mythologie, s.v. "Janus," II, 38. For his wand, see
Ovid, Fasti, VI. 165. For Janus as trickster, see ibid., I. 268:
"Ipse meae movi callidus artis opus" (Janus speaking).

[7] Henry S. Maine, Village Communities in the East and West,
192; cf. Heichelheim, Wirtschaftsgeschichte, I, 241; Thurnwald,
in Ebert's Reallexikon, s.v. "Handel," V, 86, and s.v. "Markt,"
VIII, 34–42; Aristotle, Politics, I.2.6–8.

of the city-state and the city agora. Certain Greek festivals, in which a plurality of communities participated, were known as "amphictyonies," or festivals of
the "dwellers-around"—that is, the communities which
lay around the central sacred spot. A Greek law cites
the "agora on the boundary," along with the amphictyonies, as a customary site for gatherings of neighboring
communities "in ancient times." These festivals preserved not only their original religious character, but
also their economic function: they were market festivals.[8]

Primitive trade on the boundary was deeply impreg-
nated with magical notions, remnants of which survived long after they had lost their original significance. Thus even in classical times the market of the
city agora was a sacred area and invariably contained
temples; several gods, notably Hermes, are called
agoraios, "he of the agora." But these are merely superficial features of an almost completely secularized commerce, perfunctory observance of the superstitions of
the past in a procedure which through a long evolu-
tionary process had become essentially matter-of-fact
and modern. In primitive trade, on the other hand, the
exchange is itself a ritual act. Some peculiar rituals in
the cult of Hermes, which were no longer intelligible
to the Greeks of classical times, may be explained as
vestiges of various stages in the evolution of primitive
trade.[9]

The most primitive form of trade, "silent" trade,
has features which we have already noticed in the cult

8 Gernet and Boulanger, *Le génie grec dans la religion,* 34–35;
Fougères, in Daremberg and Saglio, *s.v.* "Kome," III, 854;
Rose, *Primitive Culture in Greece,* 228; Heichelheim, *Wirtschaftsgeschichte,* I, 250; Demosthenes, XXIII. 37, with the note
in Dindorf's edition, VI, 903.
9 See Thurnwald, in Ebert's *Reallexikon, s.v.* "Handel," V, 78–
80, and "Markt," VIII, 34–35, 38; Rose, *Primitive Culture in
Greece,* 227–228; Heichelheim, *Wirtschaftsgeschichte,* I, 228.

of Hermes. In "silent" trade the parties to the exchange never meet: the seller leaves the goods in some well-known place; the buyer takes the goods and leaves the price. The exchange generally takes place at one of those points which are sacred to Hermes—a boundary point, such as a mountaintop, a river bank, a conspicuous stone, or a road junction. The object so mysteriously acquired is regarded as the gift of a supernatural being who inhabits the place, and who therefore is venerated as a magician and culture hero. For example, in the only direct evidence we have of "silent" trade between Greeks, we are told that "Lipara and Strongyle are thought to be the home of Hephaestus . . . there is an ancient tradition that anyone might bring a lump of unworked iron, and come back the next day and pick up a sword or anything else that he wanted made, provided he left a remuneration on the ground." Perhaps a folkloristic vestige of "silent" trade may be found in the Greek custom of calling any lucky find that a traveler chances upon a "gift of Hermes," ἕρμαιον. According to a Greek lexicographer the expression originated in the custom of setting out on the roadside first-fruits dedicated to Hermes, which the passers-by took and ate; that is to say, the "gifts of Hermes" were originally set out deliberately and regularly at one of the spots sacred to Hermes. If we assume, to account for the otherwise inexplicable generosity of the giver, that the passer-by was originally expected to leave a *quid pro quo* offering to the god, we have all the elements of "silent trade." [10]

[10] On the "silent" trade, see Grierson, *The Silent Trade*, 42, 44–47, 53, 56–58; Marett, *Head, Heart, and Hands*, 179–180; Schrader, *Reallexikon*, s.v. "Handel," I, 437; and scholiast on Apollonius Rhodius, *Argonautica*, IV.761. Instances of "silent" trade with the barbarians on the fringe of the classical world are recounted in Herodotus, IV.196; Philostratus, *Life of Apollonius*, VI.2; Pomponius Mela, III.7; Pliny, *Nat. Hist.*, VI.24; and Theophrastus, *Hist. Plant.*, IX.4. The isolated early Greek settlement on the Lipari Islands retained institutions after they had died out

Even in more advanced forms of primitive trade, in which the two parties are brought face to face, the act of exchange is not the simple, well-defined procedure that the term suggests to us. In modern society trade takes place within a legal framework which imposes on the two parties reciprocal recognition of their property rights, and makes the transaction dependent on mutual consent. In gentilic or tribal society, however, these principles of reciprocity and mutual consent are deprived of any possible guarantee or legal sanction by the autonomy of the familial group. Hence no juridical distinction can be drawn between legitimate and illegitimate appropriation: there is only simple appropriation. Thus in the earliest Roman codes acts of legitimate appropriation are still called thefts, *furta*. So, to enable members of different familial groups to make fair exchanges without prejudice to the autonomy of the two parties, primitive "legal" subterfuges were resorted to. "Silent" trade is one such subterfuge; mutual permission to steal is another. "In the Loyalty group," we are told, "it is common for a man to take the property of another in his presence, the presumption being that the owner will protest if he objects. The despoiled person has the equal privilege of taking what he wishes in return. In this case we have an illustration of a practice which Europeans have usually set down as stealing, but which is probably only a variation of gift exchange." Similarly at Cnossus in Crete, an island noted for its fidelity to customs long discarded on the main-

---

on the Greek mainland: primitive communism was practiced there (Diodorus, V.9). On the "gift of Hermes," see Liddell and Scott, *s.v.* ἕρμαιον; scholiast on Plato, *Phaedo*, 107C; and Hesychius, *s.v.* σῦκον ἐφ᾽ Ἑρμῆ. In a group of passers-by it was customary to divide the find equally, exclaiming "Hermes in common," κοινὸς Ἑρμῆς; see Aristotle, *Rhetoric*, II.24.2, and the note in Cope-Sandys' edition. This is the rule of equal division that prevailed in the period when property was for the most part owned by family collectivities; cf. *Odyssey*, 9.42, 549.

land, the procedure for borrowing money was simply to take it. This form of primitive exchange seems to have survived in the ritual of Hermes the Giver of Joy at Samos, at which there was general license to steal. Let us remember that "stealing" meant originally stealthy or magical action. Magic is needed to overcome the distrust of the stranger and break down the taboos on social intercourse. The exchange of goods affected by the general license to steal could only take place as a ritual sanctioned by the god of the boundary-stone.[11]

Primitive communities go beyond their own boundaries to seek not only material goods but also wives. And since the transference of women from one family group to another is beset with the same dangers and difficulties as the transference of property, the conventions surrounding marriage are similar to those governing trade. Bride-seizure, of which there are vestiges in Greek marriage customs, follows the same pattern as exchange by mutual permission to steal; it is a formality observed even when the marriage has the consent of the bride's family. In the age of village communities the festivals on the boundary were the great occasion for mating as well as for trade: hence the tradition of sexual license at these festivals even in classical times.

[11] On theft by consent as a form of exchange, see Thurn-wald, in Ebert's *Reallexikon, s.v.* "Handel," V, 74; Hoyt, *Primitive Trade*, 133–135; Glotz, *Solidarité de la famille*, p. 198, note 3; Plutarch, *Greek Questions*, 53; and Heichelheim, *Wirtschaftsgeschichte*, I, 256. For the ritual of Hermes at Samos, see Plutarch, *op. cit.*, 55. Following the interpretation of similar rituals given by Frazer (*Magic Art*, II, 310–311, and *Spirits of the Corn and of the Wild*, II, 62, 66–68), Farnell suggests (*Cults*, V, 25) that it is a fertility ritual. This suggestion is rightly rejected by Nilsson (*Griechische Feste*, 36), whose own view is that such rituals arise out of the human need to get occasional relief from conventional restraints. In each case, however, we must ask what restraints are dispensed with, and for what purpose. In the ritual of Hermes at Samos the ordinary rules governing familial property and the ordinary taboos on strangers are dispensed with for the sake of accomplishing exchange.

"Stealing" a strange woman was a magical act consummated in the rituals on the boundary. Thus Hermes came to be the master of the magic art of seduction and a patron god of marriage.[12]

Another ritual enacted in the intercommunity festivals on the boundary was the contest; the Greek word for contest, ἀγών, is derived from the same root as the word "agora" and means a "gathering." The athletic contest was also the occasion for trade, and throughout classical antiquity Hermes was one of its patron gods. In historical times a market was held in connection with the Panhellenic games, as in a county fair, the merchant being protected by the "sacred truce" proclaimed on these occasions. Originally, however, the ritual of the contest was itself the vehicle for transferring goods, as prizes; whereas in classical times the victor may have been rewarded by a simple wreath of laurel, the Homeric hero expected gold, silver, or bronze—the most highly valued objects of portable wealth. In Greek mythology brides are also sometimes disposed of by a contest among the suitors.[13]

The magico-religious ideas surrounding trade on the boundary in the age of village communities persisted, in modified form, after the village community had been absorbed by the city-state. Hermes followed trade from the perimeter of the village community to

[12] See Schrader, Reallexikon, s.v. "Raubehe," II, 215; Gernet and Boulanger, Le génie grec dans la religion, 38–41; Eitrem, in Pauly-Wissowa, VIII.774.

[13] Cf. Glotz, Solidarité de la famille, 272–282; Laum, Heiliges Geld, 57–59; Rose, Primitive Culture in Greece, 228. As a mode of transferring goods or women from one family group to another, the contest presupposes a more complex social structure than the rituals hitherto considered. The contest elevates champions above the mass of familial collectivities: the champions, that is to say the chiefs, are protagonists in the ritual drama; they also appropriate the prizes. On the other hand, when the festival on the boundary takes the form of a general license to steal, or of a general sexual orgy, there is no room for an élite; equality and collectivism pervade the procedure.

the center of the city-state, the agora, and became Hermes *agoraios*. This did not, however, result in the obliteration of his original cult centers, on the boundaries, in the wild wastelands, and on mountaintops: in the backward parts of Greece, such as Arcadia, antique monuments of the cult of Hermes, situated in the wilderness, retained a prominent place in public religion throughout the classical period. This disjunction in the location of the cult is paralleled by a disjunction in the mythological representations of Hermes current in classical times. On the one hand he is the god who was born in the mountains of rugged Arcadia, the companion of the Nymphs and other deities of the wilds, the friend of shepherds who, like the swineherd Eumaeus in the *Odyssey*, lived and worked "in a wooded spot in the uplands." On the other hand he is the friend of merchants, portrayed by Aristophanes as the very type of the "city slicker" or "man of the agora." This split personality of Hermes is explained by the history of Greek trade. In the age of village communities the boundary was the scene of both pastoral and commercial activities; when commerce moved into the city, half of Hermes became exclusively rustic and pastoral, the other half became urban and commercial.[14]

The mythology of Hermes was affected not only by the transference of the market from the boundary to the city agora, but also by the concentration of commercial activity in the hands of a specialized profession of merchants—"professional boundary-crossers," as they are called in Homer.[15] In the rituals on the boundary, exchange was a collective enterprise, and Hermes the patron god of one aspect of the life of the whole collectivity. With the absorption of the primitive familial collectivities into the larger framework of a state, economic specialization and class differentiation devel-

[14] *Odyssey*, 14.2, 435.
[15] Cf. Ebeling, *Lexikon Homericum*, *s.v.* πρηκτήρ.

oped, and the god of trade became the patron and symbol of one of the several distinct and often conflicting classes of society.

"Professional boundary-crossing" was not a monopoly of the merchant. The search for raw materials also took pioneer craftsmen into the wasteland; thus, for example, the legendary discoverers of the art of iron-smelting, the Idaean Dactyls, lived and worked in the mountains. The god of the wasteland became a patron of such enterprises: the silver-producing Mount Pangaeum was known as the haunt of Hermes, and the silver from Mount Laurium was called the gift of Hermes. Not only the search for raw materials but also the search for customers took men across the boundary. The Homeric skilled craftsman wandered from one employer's house to another's, as did the *Thetes,* or unskilled laborers, who were for that reason called vagabonds. The god of commercial intercourse became the patron of all those who sold their labor, the god who, in the words of the *Odyssey,* "grants joy and glory to the works of all mankind." The merchant, the pioneer, the craftsman, the unskilled laborer, together these form the Third Estate of Greek social history, with whose fortunes Hermes' destiny is closely bound.[16]

16 On the Idaean Dactyls, see *Phoronis,* quoted by the scholiast on Apollonius Rhodius, *Argonautica,* I.1129 (*Epicorum Graecorum Fragmenta,* ed. Kinkel, p. 211). On Hermes and the silver-mountains, see Pindar, *Pythian,* IV.177–181, and Aeschylus, *Eumenides,* 946–948. On the Homeric craftsmen and *Thetes,* see Glotz, *Ancient Greece at Work,* 29–31, 42–43, and *Iliad,* 21.444–445. On Hermes as the patron of labor, see above, page 22, note 33. Another social type which looked to Hermes the god of the wasteland for protection is represented by Autolycus, who was an outlaw; his name means "very wolf," the equivalent of the German *Vogelfrei;* he lives on Mount Parnassus; like other outlaws, he is credited with magical powers. See *Odyssey,* 19.394, 407, 457; Glotz, *Solidarité de la famille,* 23; Preller-Robert, I, 128–129, 253–254; Pauly-Wissowa, *s.v.* "Lykos" (20), XIII.2398.

CHAPTER

3

THE AGE OF HOMER

The mythology of the trickster is derived from the rituals on the boundary, rituals which originally served the needs of a culture based on autonomous familial collectivities, living in exclusive village communities. That is to say, it had in the beginning a functional relationship to this specific type of culture. As Malinowski says, "myth comes into play when rite, ceremony, or a social or moral rule demands justification, warrant of antiquity, reality, and sanctity." He also shows that precisely because myth has this "functional, cultural, and pragmatic aspect," it is continually subject to change in response to changes in human behavior.[1] It is this principle that explains the different roles which the trickster plays in different mythologies. Depending on the historical circumstances, the trickster may evolve into any one of such contrasting figures as a benevolent culture hero nearly indistinguishable from the

[1] Malinowski, *Myth in Primitive Psychology,* 28, 34, 44–59.

Supreme God, a demiurge in strong opposition to the
heavenly powers, a kind of devil counteracting the creator in every possible way, a messenger and mediator
between gods and men, or merely a Puckish figure, the
hero of comical stories.[2] The extant representations of
Hermes cover this entire range: his standard role, derived from the *Odyssey*, is that of a messenger and mediator betwen gods and men; in Hesiod's story of
Pandora he has a role resembling that of the serpent in
the Garden of Eden; in the *Homeric Hymn* he is in
revolt against the existing dispensation in heaven; occasionally he is cast in a purely Puckish role, as in the
story of how he stole his mother's clothes while she was
bathing.[3] This diversity in the representations of Hermes reflects the progressive modification of a body of
mythical material, originally shaped to answer the
needs of autonomous familial collectivities, to meet
new needs generated by changed environmental conditions.

For in the thousand years from 1500 to 500 B.C. Greece
underwent a succession of dynamic changes that al-
tered the whole pattern of Greek life—economic, political, social, and mental. This transformation was
marked by the decline of the autonomous familial collectivity, the clan and tribe, the extension of economic
and social differentiation, and the rise of kingship,
which imposed state organization upon the declining
tribe. When social differentiation had arrived at the
point of class divisions, the landed aristocracy secured
a strangle hold on the instrumentalities of state organization. Finally the regime of the landed aristocracy
was overthrown, its agrarian economy yielding to a
new economy based on trade and handicraft industry,
its political oligarchy yielding to the politics of ancient

    [2] De Vries, *The Problem of Loki*, 264.
    [3] Eitrem in Pauly-Wissowa, *s.v.* "Hermes," VIII.780–781. Cf.
Alcaeus, Frgs. 5–8 (Bergk), and Horace, *Odes*, I.10.

democracy. In this vortex of social change were crystallized other phenomena which are themselves potent catalytic agents—the development of slavery, the codification of law, the invention of money. That Greek religion could remain unaffected by environmental changes of such scope will be maintained by no one who is at all acquainted with the comparative history of religions. The essential problem of any historical study in the field of Greek religion is to show how religious institutions that were originally integral parts of the pattern of primitive tribal collectivism were adapted during successive phases of historical evolution, to changes in the Greek culture.

The earliest mythological literature of the Greeks— in Homer and Hesiod—was written at a time when their social evolution had already passed beyond the stage of tribal collectivism. Not only is it, therefore, our most valuable repository of traditions derived from that earlier era, but it also reflects the first stages of their modification in response to changes in the environment.[4]

In Homer, society is dominated by kings. The institution of kingship resulted not only in the absorption of the autonomous familial collectivities into a larger social unit, but also in the differentiation of social classes and their organization in a pyramidal structure subordinate to the kings. The most obvious and the most significant reflection of the institution of kingship in Greek mythology is the Homeric concept of Zeus as monarch of the gods. This new concept entailed a complete reorganization of the Greek Pantheon: the Olympian hierarchy as a whole was patterned after the recently experienced reality, the state, and the com-

[4] On the relation between Homer and mythical material in Homer of greater antiquity than the poems themselves, see Calhoun, "Homer's Gods: Myth and Märchen," *American Journal of Philology*, 60(1939):1–28; and Nilsson, *Homer and Mycenae*, 272–278.

ponent gods were given ranks and positions analogous
to the component orders in society. Hermes, previously
an independent and autonomous trickster, became the
subordinate of Zeus the King, his messenger and servant-in-chief. An exact parallel is found in Eddic mythology, the product of a civilization roughly comparable to the Homeric: the trickster Loki became the
faithful satellite of Thor. By a revealing coincidence
this transition of Hermes from an independent god to a
subordinate of Zeus actually takes place in the Homeric poems themselves: only in the *Odyssey* is Hermes the messenger of Zeus; in the *Iliad* that function is
performed by Iris, whereas Hermes enjoys the same in-
dependence as the other "free" gods, such as Athena
and Apollo.[5]

The subordination of Hermes to Zeus presupposes
the identification of Hermes with a definite professional group or social stratum, as Zeus is identified with
the kings, and the subordination of that stratum to the
kings. It reflects, in the first place, the evolution of the
"herald," discussed in the first chapter, who had originally been an independent magician, and as such the
earthly counterpart of Hermes the Trickster, but who
had been reduced, by the time of Homer, to the position of acolyte to the king.[6] Furthermore, by the time

[5] On the relation between Zeus's position and Mycenaean-
Homeric kingship, see Nilsson, *Mycenaean Origin of Greek
Mythology*, 221–251, and *Homer and Mycenae*, 266–272. On
Loki, see De Vries, *Problem of Loki*, 202. Nägelsbach (*Homerische Theologie*, 108–109) classifies Hermes as "unfrei" by virtue of his position in the *Odyssey*. In the *Iliad*, however, Zeus
only once orders him to do something; on another occasion the
gods merely "urge" him to follow a certain course; he releases
Ares from the brazen pot on his own initiative; in the battle of
the gods he chooses sides and takes part just as the other "free"
gods do. See *Iliad*, 5.390; 20.35, 72; 24.109, 334–338.

[6] Crome, arguing from the fact that in the *Iliad* Hermes is not
the messenger of Zeus, deduces that Hermes was not originally
the herald. See his "Kerykeia," in *Mitteilungen des deutschen*

of Homer a class of "professional boundary-crossers"—
skilled and unskilled workmen—had arisen and Hermes had become their patron. Moreover, as a result of
the institution of kingship they had become subordinate to the royal power, as the herald had. Just as the
Mycenaean palace is the archaeological reflection of
Homeric kingship, so the archaeological evidence of
the concentration of trade and industry around the
Mycenaean palace reflects the dependence of the
craftsmen on the kings at that period.[7]

The growing importance of this class of professional
workmen explains the substitution of Hermes for Iris
as the servant-in-chief of Zeus. Iris, in contrast to Hermes, was not a once-independent divinity subordinated to Zeus only when the latter was conceived as
king. She is a purely mythical figure, the Rainbow, and

---

archäologischen Instituts, Athenische Abteilung, 63(1938):125.
This inference rests on the false assumption that the herald was
never anything more nor less than a messenger. As I see it, what
is significant in the *Odyssey* is not the representation of Hermes
as herald, but the representation of the divine herald as the servant of Zeus.

[7] Glotz, *Aegean Civilization,* 150–156, 172. The fact that
Hermes appears as the servant of Zeus in the *Odyssey* but not
in the *Iliad* may be attributed to the fact that the *Odyssey* reflects a more advanced stage in the evolution of craftsmen as a
distinct social class. See Glotz, *Ancient Greece at Work,* 25.
Similarly, although the herald is already a satellite of the king
in the *Iliad,* his position is still further degraded in the *Odyssey;*
the herald Medon served the suitors against his will (*Odyssey,*
22.330–360), whereas the herald Talthybius is held in such
honor that he can intervene in the duel between Ajax and Hector on his own initiative (*Iliad,* 7.274–277); see also the wealth
of the family of heralds in *Iliad,* 10.315. The differences between the social organization depicted in the *Iliad* and in the
Odyssey are, however, differences in degree only. To explain the
qualitative difference in the mythology of the divine servant
(Iris, Hermes), it is necessary to assume a lag, which would be
natural enough, between the social change already registered in
the *Iliad* and the bringing up to date of the mythology in the
Odyssey.

as such was from the beginning a member of the
household of Zeus the Sky-god. Iris' service to her father Zeus is patterned after the service rendered by the
junior members of a family to their elders; it is the
same service that is performed by Nausicaä and other
unmarried daughters in Homer. Iris eventually becomes the personal handmaiden of Zeus's wife Hera,
just as in a later age of Greece Nausicaä was confined
to the women's quarters and her function limited to
the work supervised by the matron of the house.
Hermes, on the other hand, represents service obtained from beyond the boundary, from outside the
family. The substitution of Hermes for Iris, which
takes place when Zeus becomes the head of a state instead of the head of a family, thus reflects the novel
feature in the economy of the royal households—their
reliance on hired labor.[8]

[8] On Iris, see Preller-Robert, I, 498, and Weicker, in Pauly-
Wissowa, *s.v.* "Iris," IX.2041. Their explanations of the change
in Iris' position are not satisfactory. According to Preller-Robert,
the change was the result of the degradation of Iris to the position of handmaiden to Hera. This is a circular argument, since,
as Weicker points out, it was the intrusion of Hermes that led
to the degradation of Iris. Weicker attributes the change to the
"growing importance" of Hermes. This begs the question; what
sort of importance and why? Murray (*Five Stages of Greek Religion*, 76–77) offers a more precise explanation: "Hermes was
originally, outside Homer, an upright stone. . . . Now this
phallic stone was quite unsuitable to Homer. It was not decent;
it was not quite human. . . . In the *Iliad* Hermes is simply removed, and a beautiful creation or tradition, Iris, the rainbow
goddess, takes his place as the messenger from heaven to earth.
In the *Odyssey* he is admitted, but so changed and castigated
that no one would recognize the old Herm in the beautiful and
gracious youth who performs the god's messages." The miscon-
ceptions underlying this type of Homeric criticism, with its assumption that the poets of the Greek epic and their audience
"felt somewhat as Mr. Murray and we about divinity," have
been thoroughly exposed by G. M. Calhoun. See his article,
"The Higher Criticism on Olympus," in the *American Journal of
Philology*, 58(1937):257–274. A cardinal fallacy in Murray's
argument is the assumption that before Homer there was no anthropomorphic Greek mythology, only *mana*. This involves him

in fantastic self-contradictions: Iris takes over Hermes' original function of messenger because Hermes is not anthropomorphic; we are asked to believe that before Homer the Greeks attributed the function of messenger to an "upright stone." Murray's theory also contradicts the facts: Hermes appears in the *Iliad* in a form that is both decent and human, though not as messenger.

CHAPTER

4

THE AGE OF HESIOD

According to the story of Pandora in Hesiod's *Works and Days,* Zeus, determined to visit sorrow on men because Prometheus had stolen fire from heaven and given it to them, has Hephaestus fashion a woman out of clay, Athena equip her with handicraft skill, Aphrodite with beauty, and Hermes with "the mind of a cur and a stealthy disposition." Zeus calls her Pandora because all the gods have endowed her with gifts. Pandora is conducted by Hermes to Epimetheus, who accepts her, against the advice of his brother Prometheus. Then she takes the lid off the jar in which her gifts are contained. Whereas men have lived up to this time free from ills or toil or sickness, now "the earth is full of ills, and the sea is also full of them," and only Hope remains in the jar.[1]

Hermes, though he is only one of several gods from whom Pandora received her equipment, and although

1 Hesiod, *Works and Days,* 42–104.

her creation was initiated by Zeus, has a special responsibility for the catastrophe. Pandora opened the
jar with malice aforethought: "she had in her mind bit-
ter sorrows for men"; and her maliciousness—"the
mind of a cur and a stealthy disposition"—was bestowed on her by Hermes. The opening of the jar has
the same fateful import as the eating of the forbidden
fruit in the Garden of Eden; Hermes plays a role analogous to that of the serpent who tempted Eve. Like
Hermes, the serpent was a trickster, "more subtil than
any beast of the field"; in both myths the trickster appears as a satanic character.[2]

Hesiod's concept of Hermes as a sinister figure marks
a new stage in the evolution of the mythology of the
god. As we saw in Chapter I, the tricksterishness of
which Hermes was the symbol was a source of benefits
to humanity: the trickster is identical with the culture
hero. In Homer, as contrasted with Hesiod, Hermes is
actually said to be the god who is friendliest to mankind. The ends to which his trickery is directed are in
all cases benevolent; the "stealthy disposition" which
Homer says Hermes gave to Autolycus is represented
as an unquestionable asset, whereas the same gift,
given to Pandora, is a curse.[3]

Why has Hesiod blackened Hermes' character? To
answer this question we must analyze Pandora, for
Hermes is sinister only as the cause of evil symbolized
by Pandora.

Pandora, as the misogynist Hesiod takes pains to
emphasize, is a woman, and the "stealthy disposition"
that Hermes has given her refers to the bewitching
guiles of sex appeal. In his *Theogony,* where he tells a

[2] *Works and Days,* 95. Cf. W. Headlam, "Prometheus and the
Garden of Eden," *Classical Quarterly,* 28(1934):63–71.

[3] See *Iliad,* 24.334–335. Compare the degeneration of Loki
from the faithful companion of Thor and Odin to a kind of
Satan in the myth of Balder. De Vries, *Problem of Loki,* 202,
264, 293–296.

slightly different version of the same myth, Hesiod describes the woman fashioned out of clay by Hephaestus as the prototype of womankind, and explicitly formulates the idea that Zeus's revenge for Prometheus' theft of fire consisted in presenting mankind with "the accursed race of womankind," "a trick which men could not resist." In so far as Pandora in the *Works and Days* is, like her unnamed counterpart in the *Theogony*, a personification of the female sex, Hesiod's negative attitude toward Hermes, the god of sexual appeal and marriage, may be attributed to his profound misogynism.[4]

Pandora is, however, more than a personification of the female sex. A writer who, like Hesiod, uses mythology to illustrate his own moral and social philosophy can find more than one meaning in a single myth. Hesiod introduces the myth of Pandora at the beginning of his *Works and Days* to demonstrate to his good-for-nothing brother, to whom the poem is addressed, the necessity for work. The necessity for work, and not, as in the *Theogony*, the "accursed race of women," is represented to be Zeus's revenge on mankind for Prometheus' theft of fire: "for the gods have hidden away from men the means of existence; otherwise you would easily do enough work in a day to supply you for a full year even without working. . . . But Zeus in the anger of his heart hid it, because the crafty Prometheus deceived him." The opening of Pandora's jar has the same consequences as the eating of the forbidden fruit in the Garden of Eden: "And unto Adam he said, Because thou hast hearkened unto the voice of thy wife, and

---

[4] See Hesiod, *Theogony*, 570–612. The misogynist motif is also present in the *Works and Days*: see line 94. Hesiod's misogynism—an attitude which differentiates his from the Homeric outlook—is the result of the social conditions under which he lived. The diatribe against women in the *Theogony* (lines 590–612) reveals that his misogynism stems from the difficulty he has faced, as a poor farmer, in supporting a wife.

hast eaten of the tree, of which I commanded thee, saying, Thou shalt not eat of it: cursed is the ground for thy sake; in sorrow shalt thou eat of it all the days of thy life. . . . In the sweat of thy face shalt thou eat bread." Like the story of the Garden of Eden, Hesiod's myth contrasts man's present fate with a lost Paradise. Immediately after the myth of Pandora follows the myth of the five generations of men; the opening of Pandora's jar marks the transition from the golden generation, who "lived without sorrow or toil," to the iron generation, who "never rest from labour or sorrow." According to Hesiod, this change in the condition of men corresponds to a dynastic change in heaven: during the Golden Age Cronus was king of the gods; now Zeus reigns in his place. Pandora symbolizes the earthly dispensation that corresponds to the Olympian dynasty of gods over which Zeus is king: Hesiod says she was called Pandora "because all the Olympians gave her a gift for men," or, as some translate it, "because all the Olympians gave her as a gift to men"; in any case the essence of Pandora is that she embodies the gifts of the Olympian gods. The "gifts of the gods" is a religious formula referring to the manner in which men obtain their livelihood. Pandora symbolizes living conditions in the age of the iron generation, which Hesiod identifies with his own times.[5]

---

[5] *Works and Days,* 42–48, 81–82; compare 90–93 with 112–115, and 103–104 with 174–178. On the translation of lines 81–82 of *Works and Days,* see Robert, "Pandora," *Hermes,* 49 (1914):25–27, and Rzach, "Hesiodos," *Jahresbericht über die Fortschritte der klassischen Altertumswissenschaft,* 119 (1924): 49. The standard authorities interpret the myth of Pandora as inspired by Hesiod's misogynism; see Weizsacker, in Roscher, *Lexikon der Mythologie, s.v.* "Pandora," III, 1523, 1528; Robert, "Pandora," *op. cit.,* 24; Schwartz, "Prometheus bei Hesiod," *Sitzungsberichte der Königlich Preussischen Akademie der Wissenschaften, Berlin,* 1915, p. 142; and Nilsson, *History of Greek Religion,* 184. Such an interpretation ignores the intimate connection between the myths and the social philosophy of the *Works and Days;* see Meyer, "Hesiods Erga," *Kleine Schriften,*

The gifts of the gods, Hesiod is saying, are a mixed blessing—in the Greek phrase, "gifts that are no gifts." "Because men have fire, I will give them an evil to go with it," says Zeus as he orders the manufacture of Pandora. The ambivalence of the gifts of the gods is manifest not only in Pandora's relation to fire, but also in the nature of Pandora herself: she was called Pandora "because all the Olympians gave her as *a gift, a sorrow* to mortal men." Zeus prophesies that men will delight in her, "embracing their own destruction." [6] The same idea is present in the motif of the jar, the opening of which is responsible for the evil in the world.

There has been much controversy about the contents of this celebrated jar. Hesiod's description of the consequences that ensued upon the opening of it suggests that it was a jar of evils, which escaped and spread over the world. On the other hand, there is a tradition, going back as early as the poet Theognis (sixth century B.C.), that the jar contained good things which escaped and were lost. Furthermore, jars were used by the Greeks for storing *goods*, mostly food—the "means of existence" which Hesiod says the gods have hidden from mankind; and Hope, who remained in the jar, can hardly be interpreted as an evil. Hence some scholars have concluded that the text has been tampered with so as to obliterate an original concept of the

---

II, 18–19, 28–29, 32–33; W. Fuss, *Versuch einer Analyse von Hesiods* Ἔργα καὶ Ἡμέραι (Leipzig, 1910); P. Mason, "Hésiode: La Composition des Travaux et des Jours," *Revue des études anciennes,* 14(1912):329–356; and Jaeger, *Paideia,* I, 63–64. Hesiod's subject in the *Theogony* is *human* origins, in the *Works and Days* cultural* origins: in the *Theogony* the artificial woman is said to be the first woman, in the *Works and Days* she is not; in the *Works and Days* she is said to be the cause of the evil in the world, in the *Theogony* she is not; only in the *Works and Days* is she given the name Pandora, with the special etymology which is so appropriate to the symbol of culture, and quite inappropriate to the symbol of womankind.

6 *Works and Days,* 57, 82, 58.

contents of the jar as good things, and to introduce the mention of the evils. Others have suggested that the jar contained some things that were good and some that were evil.[7] The puzzling contradictions in the passage are explained if, in line with Hesiod's fundamental idea, we interpret the contents of the jar as both good and evil—not some good and some evil, but all a "gift" that was at the same time a "sorrow." Hesiod is exploiting the concept, present in many mythologies, of a receptacle whose magic contents are an asset if rightly handled, a liability if they get out of control. The sack containing the winds, which Aeolus gave to Odysseus, is an example. Hesiod's model was the ritual of the "Opening of the Jars" in the Dionysiac festival of the Anthesteria. This ritual was a ceremonial opening of the jars of new wine; the new wine was, according to Plutarch, a *pharmakon*: the word, which is untranslatable, signifies a thing fraught with special magic powers which can produce either favorable or unfavorable effects, according to the circumstances. He goes on to say that "it appears that in olden times they poured a libation from it before drinking it, and prayed that the use of the *pharmakon* might be without hurt to themselves, and a source of salvation." Pandora's "Opening of the Jar" inaugurates not a new cycle of seasons, but a new age, in which the sinister powers of the gift of the gods were unfolded.[8]

[7] For various views on the contents of Pandora's jar, see Rzach, in Pauly-Wisowa, *s.v.* "Hesiodos," VIII.1181; Robert, "Pandora," *op. cit.*, 31; Wilamowitz, *Hesiodos Erga*, 51–52; Gow, "Elpis and Pandora," *Essays and Studies Presented to William Ridgeway*, edited by E. C. Quiggen, 99–104; P. Girard, "Le Mythe de Pandore dans la poésie hésiodique," *Revue des études grecques*, 22(1909):217–230; Schwartz, "Prometheus bei Hesiod," *op. cit.*, 141–142; and Guarducci, "Leggende dell' antica Grecia relative all' origine dell' umanità," *Memorie della reala Accademia dei Lincei, classe di scienze morali, storiche e filologiche*, 2(1926):446–448. See also Theognis, 1135–1150; Babrius, *Fabulae*, 58; *Anthologia Palatina*, X. 71.

[8] For the general mythological concept, see *Odyssey*, 10.19–

Hesiod's doctrine is that the culture of his own times is a curse rather than a blessing. What features in that culture is he repudiating? Further study of Pandora gives us the answer. Hesiod did not invent Pandora; he adapted an existent myth to his own purposes. She was originally a figure of the earth-goddess type, the original meaning of the name being "the all-giver." Nor did Hesiod invent the connection between Pandora and Prometheus (or Epimetheus); he drew upon a myth which told of Pandora's liberation from a prison-house below ground by Prometheus armed with a mallet, and her subsequent marriage with him. Nineteenth-century scholars, in accordance with their disposition to inter-

---

27, 46–49; see also the comparative material referred to above, p. 13, note 19. The analogy with the "Opening of the Jars" was first pointed out by Jane Harrison in "Pandora's Box," *Journal of Hellenic Studies,* 20(1900):99–114. She was, however, under the misapprehension that the jars opened at this ceremony contained the ghosts of the dead (κῆρες), which, according to her, suggested to Hesiod the concept of a jar that released maleficent powers (κῆρας, *Works and Days,* 92). For the correct interpretation of the ceremony, see Farnell, *Cults,* V, 221–223; Deubner, *Attische Feste,* 94; and Plutarch, *Moralia,* 655F. The κῆρας of *Works and Days,* 92, are the evils that come in the train of material progress: cf. Pindar, Frg. 289 (ed. Bowra), κῆρες ὀλβο-θρέμμονες; Theopompus, Frg. 332 (ed. Jacoby)—the Spartan ephors exorcise (ἀποδιοπομπεῖσθαι) all the gold and silver in the city ὥσπερ κῆρας ἐπαγωγίμους; Plato, *Laws,* 937D: πολλῶν ὄντων καὶ καλῶν ἐν τῷ τῶν ἀνθρώπων βίῳ, τοῖς πλείστοις αὐτῶν οἷον κῆρες ἐπιπεφύκασιν. In *Works and Days,* 94–95, where Hesiod says, "But the woman, taking off the great lid, scattered," the object of the verb "scattered" is left undefined so as to leave the reader with two impressions: (1) that the jar contained the usual contents of a jar, i.e., something valuable, and (2) that at the same time it was a source of evils. Those scholars who say that the jar contained evils supply an object from the evils mentioned in the genitive case three lines earlier—an expedient open to serious grammatical objections. Those who say that the jars contained goods are forced to assume the loss from the text of some lines in which the contents were defined. On Hesiod's general point of view, see Meyer, "Hesiods Erga," *op. cit.,* 32, where he says that Hesiod is as hostile to culture as Rousseau; the same attitude characterizes several of the prophets of the Old Testament, with whom Meyer compares him.

pret Greek myths as nature myths, have regarded Prometheus as the symbol of solar fire, which releases the
bounty of the earth from the winter prison. But the
vase-paintings which show Satyrs (the manual laborers
of Greek mythology) and even plain ordinary men releasing the earth-goddess from her subterranean prison
prove that Prometheus with his mallet—a tool used by
the Greeks for breaking up the soil—represents the fertility-promoting action not of a natural element, but of
human labor and skill. Originally, therefore, Pandora
symbolized the bounty of earth, and Prometheus (or
Epimetheus) the art of agriculture. Contrast Pandora
in Hesiod. She is an artifact, manufactured by the
craftsman god Hephaestus; she is given to mankind
along with Promethean fire, which is the symbol of metallurgy; the gods involved in her creation include the
leading artificers and culture heroes of the Greek Pantheon (Hephaestus, Athena, Hermes) and the leading
artificer hero, Prometheus. Pandora in Hesiod is the
symbol of handicraft culture.[9]

---

[9] On the origin of Pandora, see Robert, "Pandora," *op. cit.*,
17–26; Harrison, *Prolegomena to the Study of Greek Religion*,
277–278; Guarducci, "Leggende," *op. cit.*, 438–441. The crucial
evidence is the vase-painting Ashmolean Museum 525 (*Corpus
Vasorum Antiquorum*, Oxford 1 [Great Britain 3], plate 21, figs.
1 and 2); cf. the similar vases enumerated *ibid.*, pp. 18–19. For
the vase-paintings of the release of the earth-goddess, see
E. Langlotz, "Epimetheus," *Die Antike*, 6(1930):1–14. Robert
ascribes Hesiod's changes in the nature of Pandora to his own
misogynism: for the concept of Earth as the mother of the
human race Hesiod substituted the concept of the evil artificial
woman as the prototype of womankind. Apart from the general
objections to the misogynist interpretation of Pandora (see above,
note 5), it is clear that Hesiod never rejected the tradition that
Earth was the mother of all: that is the role of Gaia in the
Theogony, to which an allusion is made in *Works and Days*,
108, where it is said that both men and gods have the same
origin. This is the essence of the concept of the Earth as mother
of all; see Pindar, *Nemean*, VI.1–2; Wilamowitz, *Hesiodos Erga*,
54. Hence it cannot be objected that in the *Theogony* Gaia is
the mother of the gods only. Furthermore, whenever the Earth
is referred to as the mother of the human (or the divine) race,

Hermes appears in the myth of Pandora in his traditional role of culture hero: as a god of craftsmanship he participates in the creation of Pandora; as "giver of good things" he inspires Pandora to open the jar. Hesiod, because he repudiates the culture with which the god is identified, represents the culture hero as a mischief-maker responsible for the evil in Creation.

The age of Hesiod (the seventh century B.C.) was an age of crisis, born of the conflict between two social systems, the old order of familial collectivism and a new economy based on the profit motive and the division of labor. The new economy, which was promoted by the growth of handicraft industry and commerce in the nascent centers of urban civilization, is reflected in the development of the city agora into a market-place, which took place in Hesiod's time. The champions of the new economy, and of its ethic of acquisitive individualism, were the Third Estate of merchants and craftsmen, who had already crystallized into a distinct social class in the Homeric age, and who were now successfully emancipating themselves from their previous dependent status. In Hesiod's words, "neighbor vies with neighbor as he speeds on the road to wealth . . . and potter is angry with potter, and car-

---

she is called Ge, or Gaia, never Pandora; cf. Plato, *Menexenus,* 237E; Asius, quoted by Pausanias, VIII.1.2. In terms of an agricultural economy, the Earth is considered as (1) the Giver of all, and (2) the Mother of all; in terms of a handicraft economy, (1) the Giver of all (culture) is identified with craftsmanship, and (2) human beings are regarded as artifacts in origin. A Hesiodic fragment (Frg. 268, Rzach) represents Prometheus as fashioning men out of clay; see Guarducci, "Leggende," *op. cit.,* 421–432. In the *Theogony* Hesiod tells the myth as a story of human origins; in the *Works and Days* he tells the same myth as a story of cultural origins. On the theory of Schwartz ("Prometheus bei Hesiod," *op. cit.,* 144) that the fire stolen by Prometheus is the sacrificial fire and not the fire used in metallurgy, see S. M. Adams, "Hesiod's Pandora," *Classical Review,* 46 (1932):194, and Schmid-Stählin, *Geschichte der griechischen Literatur,* Part I, Vol. I, p. 247.

penter with carpenter." The new ethic of acquisitive individualism conflicted with the traditional morality which the Greeks called Themis—the body of customs and laws inherited from the age of familial collectivism. In this conflict Hesiod is wholeheartedly on the side of Themis; he is the first nostalgic reactionary in Western civilization. In his view acquisitive individualism is "robbery," a concept which is based not on a practical casuistry distinguishing permissible from impermissible gain, but on a rejection in principle of the profit motive, as is the sin of avarice in the ethic of the medieval schoolmen. "Robbery," "Shamelessness," "Force," "Strife," are the harsh realities of life in the iron generation; "Shame" and "Justice," the daughters of Themis, the ideal patterns of human behavior, exist only in heaven. Hesiod recommends agriculture as the best way of life because it offers the maximum self-sufficiency, the maximum isolation from the new economy; his calendar of *Works and Days* is designed to make the farmer as self-sufficient as possible, as independent as possible of the craftsman, even when such a policy is economically irrational. Hesiod is an isolationist: "it is better to stay at home, since the outside world is noxious"; he firmly turns his back on the new commercial culture.[10]

---

[10] *Works and Days*, 23–25, 182–201, 220–224, 365. Heichelheim (*Wirtschaftsgeschichte*, I, 262) takes Hesiod's concept of robbery (ἄρπαξ) at its face value, as referring to plundering raids in the Homeric style. But in *Works and Days*, line 38, the term is applied to wealth gained by legal chicanery; in lines 320–324 it includes wealth obtained by verbal chicanery and as a result of immoral desire for profit (κέρδος); "Robbery" is equated with "Shamelessness" and "Violence," and contrasted with "Shame" and "Justice"; compare lines 323 and 352, 324 and 359, 321 and 192. "Robbery" is any acquisition which violates the rules of Themis; hence in line 356 "robbery" is contrasted with "gift-giving"—that is to say, the archaic form of commerce by mutual exchange of gifts, which was still practiced in the Homeric age. On the economic developments of the Hesiodic age, see Heichelheim, *Wirtschaftsgeschichte*, I, 249–250, 273–274; Glotz,

Hermes' gift of a "stealthy disposition," which refers
to the guiles of sex appeal when applied to Pandora as
woman, refers to the ethics of acquisitive individualism
when applied to Pandora as the symbol of the new culture. By the time of Hesiod the element of magic in
primitive trade and craftsmanship, which was the original basis for the concept of the trickster as culture
hero, had disappeared; the rituals of Hermes preserved
the original forms, but only as cultural vestiges, devoid
of their original function and meaning. At the same
time that Hermes' vitality as culture hero was renewed
through his connection with the new commercial culture, the trickery associated with his name acquired a
new meaning from the same context: the epithet
κερδῷος, which originally meant "tricky," came to mean
"good for securing profit." Hesiod uses "trickery" as
well as "robbery" as abusive terms to describe the ethic
of acquisitive individualism: "wealth that is not the
fruit of robbery but is god-given, is much better. For if
a man seizes great riches by force with his hands, or if
he gets his plunder through his tongue, as often hap-
pens when gain (κέρδος) deceives men's senses, and
shamelessness tramples down shame, the gods soon
blot him out." "God-given" wealth is wealth acquired
according to the laws of Themis; the divine is equated
with the ideal, which is in contradiction with the real.
It follows that wealth given by Hermes is not "god-
given." Hesiod's dualistic philosophy infects his theol-
ogy; Hermes, the symbol of the immoral reality, is reduced to the rank of a satan.[11]

Ancient Greece at Work, 69–72; and A. A. Trever, "The Age of
Hesiod," Classical Philology, 19(1924):157–168. On Hesiod's
attitude toward the new commercial culture, see P. Waltz, "Les
Artisans et leur vie en Grèce: I. Le Siècle d'Hésiode," Revue
historique, 177 (1914):14–18; Fuss, op. cit., 29.

[11] Works and Days, 320–325. Note that in the Theogony,
where the artificial creature is the prototype of womankind,
Hermes is not mentioned. Furthermore, the Works and Days in-

Hesiod expounds the conflict between the trickster-god and the principles of Themis in the myth of Metis, told in the *Theogony*. Hesiod says that Zeus took as his first wife Metis (Intelligence), the wisest of the gods; but when she was about to give birth to Athena, he swallowed Metis, because the ancient divinities Earth and Sky warned him that her progeny might wrest his kingdom from him: Athena, her first-born, was destined to be the equal of her father in strength and in wisdom, and after Athena she was destined to bear a son who would be king of gods and of men. Metis remains in Zeus's belly, giving him knowledge of good and evil, and he took Themis (Moral Law) as his wife, and she brought forth Good Order, Justice, and Peace.[12]

Metis, Intelligence, is represented as ambivalent, like Pandora: on the one hand she is an asset that Zeus retains in his belly; on the other hand her progeny constitutes a potential threat to Zeus. Hesiod contrasts the dangerous Metis with Themis, whom he exalts at the expense of Metis: Themis replaces Metis as Zeus's wife, and her children, as a result of Zeus's timely swallowing of his first wife, take precedence as Zeus's first legitimate offspring.[13]

---

troduces Aphrodite, who too is unmentioned in the *Theogony*, to endow the woman with "beauty and desire"; thus in the *Works and Days* it is really Aphrodite who supplies the woman with sex appeal, and some other meaning must be found for Hermes' gift. Note also that Athena, who in the *Theogony* simply clothes the woman, in the *Works and Days* teaches her handicraft.

[12] *Theogony*, 886–902.

[13] Most scholars have not taken seriously the idea that the progeny of Metis constituted a threat to Zeus; see Meyer, "Hesiods Erga," *op. cit.*, 64; Farnell, *Cults*, I, 285. Some go so far as to condemn as spurious the passage in the *Theogony* (lines 891–899) which refers to the dangerous progeny of Metis; see Wilamowitz, "Athena," *Sitzungsberichte der Preussischen Akademie, Berlin*, 1921, pp. 957–958; Kruse, in Pauly-Wissowa, *s.v.* "Metis," XV.1409. The correct interpretation is indicated

What sort of "Intelligence" is it that Hesiod contrasts with "Moral Law"? It is the intelligence or knowledge of the skilled craftsman. The personification Metis is embedded in a complex of mythology dealing with metallurgy and divine and heroic metallurgists. Athena is not only a warrior maiden, but also a goddess of craftsmanship—Hesiod uses the periphrasis "Athena's servant" for a carpenter. Her martial prowess she owes to her father Zeus; her skill at handicraft is derived from her mother Metis, as is indicated in the myth which makes Athena the daughter of Metis by one of those mythical smiths the Cyclopes. Metis' unnamed son is identifiable by an enumeration of the gods who are represented as excelling in the quality of *metis:* they are, apart from Zeus and Athena, Prometheus (the second half of whose name contains the root), Hephaestus, and Hermes—the culture heroes of Greek mythology. These three are the gods who finally succeed in bringing about Athena's birth, by wielding an axe to release her from Zeus's head. No single one of these gods can be identified with Metis' unnamed son; Hesiod's thought is that the culture hero type of god is a subversive force that must be suppressed in favor of a reassertion of the principles of the Moral Law. The dangerous Metis and the contrasting Themis correspond to what we call science and morality when, in a pessimistic vein similar to Hesiod's, we say that the progress of morality has not kept pace with the progress of science.[14]

---

by Schmid-Stählin in *Geschichte der griechischen Literatur,* Part I, Vol. I, p. 281.

[14] On the connection between Metis and metallurgy, see Gruppe, *Griechische Mythologie und Religionsgeschichte,* II, 1211–1213. On Athena as the goddess of craftsmanship, see Hesiod, *Works and Days,* 430, and Buchholz, *Homerischen Realien,* III, 138–140. On Athena's descent from a Cyclops, see Kruse, in Pauly-Wissowa, *s.v.* "Metis," XV.1410. For Athena

As an attribute of the culture hero *metis* is hardly distinguishable in meaning from the "trickery" which implies skilled expertness. In fact the root usually has the connotation of "guile," and should therefore be added to the list of words which show the interpenetration of the notions of "trickery" and "skill." *Metis,* however, has other denotations than intelligence in craftsmanship. Homer uses the root to refer not only to the technical skill of Hephaestus, but also to the shrewdness of Odysseus and the sagacity of Zeus: as applied to Odysseus or Zeus, it is an attribute of kings; in Homer the royal and the technical *metis* are not clearly differentiated. Hesiod inherited the equivocation, stereotyped in the traditional epithets applied to the gods and in myths which linked the personification Metis both with the king and with the craftsmen among the gods; at the same time his moral and social philosophy demanded that Zeus be aligned with Themis against Metis. In his clumsy myth he reconciles tradition with his own conscience by discriminating between Metis herself, who represents the royal *metis* and remains with Zeus, and her unwelcome offspring, who represent the technical *metis.* A later age solved the difficulty by simply abandoning the inconvenient

---

πολύμητις, see *Homeric Hymns,* XXVIII.2, and *Odyssey,* 13.299. For Prometheus ἀγκυλομήτης, see Hesiod, *Theogony,* 546. For Hephaestus πολύμητις, see *Homeric Hymns,* XX.1, and *Iliad,* 21.355. For Hermes αἱμυλομήτης, see *Homeric Hymn to Hermes,* 13. On the release of Athena from the head of Zeus by Hephaestus, Prometheus, and Hermes, see Preller-Robert, I, 189, and Malten, in Pauly-Wissowa, *s.v.* "Hephaistos," VIII.313, 347. Cf. the association of Athena, Prometheus, and Hephaestus in the festivals of the Athenian metal-workers; see Farnell, *Cults,* V, 377–386, and Malten, *op. cit.,* VIII.349. Wilamowitz denies that it is as a goddess of craftsmanship that Athena is connected with Metis and Prometheus, but he offers no adequate counter-arguments. "Hephaistos," *Nachrichten von der Königlichen Gesellschaft der Wissenschaften zu Göttingen, Philologisch-historische Klasse,* 1895, p. 240.

tradition: Pindar firmly asserts that Themis was Zeus's
first wife.[15]

[15] See Ebeling, *Lexicon Homericum*, *s.v.* μῆτις; Wilamowitz,
Heimkehr des Odysseus, p. 190, note 1. For Pindar's version of
Zeus's first marriage, see Frg. 10 (ed. Bowra). It is inconsistent
of Wilamowitz ("Athena," *op. cit.*, 957–958), who himself
showed in his *Isyllos von Epidaurus* how Pindar contradicts
Hesiod's mythology when it does not correspond with Pindaric
ethics, to argue from this passage that Pindar did not use a *Theogony* which named Metis as Zeus's first wife.

CHAPTER

5

THE *HOMERIC HYMN TO HERMES*

The *Homeric Hymn to Hermes* is the canonical document for all subsequent descriptions and discussions of Hermes the Thief. Before we analyze the component elements in its synthesis of the mythology of the god, we must first survey the plot of the *Hymn* as a whole.

A brief preface (lines 1–19) informs us of the subject of the *Hymn*—Hermes, the son of Zeus and Maia, whom Zeus used to visit for as long as he could while his lawful wife Hera was sleeping.[1] The fruit of this clandestine union was an unusual child who was shifty, cunning, and thievish, and highly precocious: on the very day of his birth he stole the cattle of Apollo. The rest of the *Hymn,* apart from five valedictory lines at

[1] See Radermacher, *Der homerische Hermeshymnus,* p. 59, note on lines 7 and 8.

the end, is a narrative of the events of this exciting day.

As he crossed the threshold of the cave on Mount Cyllene in Arcadia where his mother lived, he found a tortoise. Realizing at once the use to which he could put this find, he fashioned it into a lyre, thus becoming the inventor of the tortoise-shell lyre. After accompanying himself on his new instrument in a song about the love of Zeus and Maia—by which he was begotten —he left the lyre in his cradle and, feeling hungry, proceeded on his way after the cattle of Apollo (lines 20–62). These he found in the region of Mount Olympus, with the cattle of the rest of the gods. It was nighttime by now. Hermes drove away fifty cows of Apollo's herd, taking many precautions to throw the pursuit off the scent: he drove the cattle backward so that their footprints would point to the meadow from which he had stolen them, and he made himself a pair of sandals so constructed as to cover up his own footprints. On his way back to Arcadia he met only one person, an old man working in his vineyard at Onchestus in Boeotia; Hermes advised him that if he knew what was good for him he would keep his mouth shut about what he had seen (lines 63–93).

Upon reaching the ford across the Alpheus (in Elis) he foddered the cattle and put them away in a cave. Then he collected some wood and lit a fire with firesticks, thus becoming the inventor of this method of creating fire. Next he dragged two of the cows out of the cave, threw them on the ground, and made a sacrifice, dividing them into twelve portions. After throwing away his sandals, he smoothed the sand and returned to his mother's home on Mount Cyllene without being observed. He entered the house through the keyhole, like a wisp of cloud, and nestled down in his cradle, tucking the tortoise-shell lyre under his arm, like a baby with his toy (lines 94–153). But he had not fooled his mother. She asked him what he had been up to, and she took a pessimistic view of his chances of getting away with his first venture on a career of thievery. "Alas," she sighed, "when your father begot you, he begot a deal of trouble for mortal men and for the immortal gods." Hermes' reply was definitely in character: "Why do you try to scare me as if I were nothing but a silly child? I shall follow the career that offers the best opportunities, for I must look after my own interests and yours. It is intolerable that we alone of the immortals should have to live in this dreary cave, receiving neither offerings nor prayers. Would it not be better to spend our days in ease and affluence like the rest of the gods? I am going to get the same status in cult as Apollo. If my father does not give it to me, I will become the prince of thieves. If Apollo hunts me down, I will go and plunder his shrine at Delphi; there is plenty of gold there—just you see" (lines 154–181).

Meanwhile Apollo was in pursuit of the thief. Aided by information from the old man of Onchestus and by the flight of a bird—Apollo was a master at interpreting such omens—he identified the culprit and arrived at Maia's home. When Hermes saw him, he curled up in his cradle and pretended to be asleep. Apollo searched the place for his cattle. Failing to find them, he brusquely ordered Hermes to tell where they were. "Why, son of Leto," Hermes asked, "what means this rough language? I never even saw your cattle. Do I look like a cattle-raider? I am only two days old, and all I am interested in is sleep and warm baths and my mother's milk." "You certainly have won the title of prince of thieves," replied Apollo, as he picked Hermes up. But Hermes also knew about omens; as he was being lifted up, he let out an omen, "an unfortunate servant of the belly, an impudent messenger," and sneezed for good luck. Apollo dropped him at once.

After further mutual recriminations, the matter was referred to Zeus for judgment (lines 182–324). "And
what is this fine prize you have carried off?" Zeus asks
Apollo as he sees him carrying a new-born baby under
his arm. "It is not fair to accuse me of carrying things
off," Apollo replied; "he is the thief, and a most cunning one too." Then he told Zeus about Hermes' de-
vices for covering up his traces, and how he had pretended ignorance about the stolen cattle. At this point
Hermes spoke in his own defense. "Father," he said,
"you know I cannot tell a lie. He came to our house
looking for some cattle and began threatening me—
and he is grown-up, whereas I was born only yester-
day. I swear by the gates of heaven that I never drove
the cattle to our house, and that I never stepped across
our threshold. I will get even with this fellow for so
violently arresting me; you must defend the cause of
the weak and helpless." Zeus laughed heartily when he
heard his dishonest son's ingenious denials; but his
judgment was that Hermes should show Apollo where
the cattle were (lines 325–396).

So Hermes took Apollo to the ford across the Alpheus and drove the cattle out of the cave where he
had hidden them. Outside the cave were two cowhides
which Hermes had laid out on a rock after the sacrifice.
Apollo was amazed that a new-born baby should have
been able to skin two cows. "You don't need to grow
up," he said, as he began to twine a rope of withies to
lead away the cattle.[2] But Hermes did not want him to
lead away the cattle; so, to Apollo's amazement, he
used his magic powers to make the withies twine over
the cattle and take root in the ground. He then pro-

[2] I interpret the object which Apollo wants to bind, men-
tioned in the lacuna after line 409, as the cattle (see Allen and
Halliday, *The Homeric Hymns*, 330–332), not as the lyre (see
Radermacher, *op. cit.*, 145–147). See Appendix B.

duced the lyre and began playing on it, singing of the origin of the gods and of the offices assigned to each. Apollo was overcome by the sweetness of the music. "What you have there is worth fifty cattle," he said to Hermes; "I know about music; I accompany the Muses when they dance to the sound of flutes; but never have I heard music such as this, music full of invitations to gaiety and love and sleep. Tell me the secret of your instrument; I will see to it, I swear, that you get a position of wealth and honor among the gods." Hermes replied with characteristic shrewdness, "I am not selfish; it would be a pleasure to teach you the secret of my instrument, just as Zeus taught you the art of prophecy.[3] It is indeed a marvelous instrument in the hands of a true artist. In return you must be generous and share your patronage over cattle with me." And so a bargain was struck: Hermes received the neatherd's staff from Apollo, and Apollo received the lyre from Hermes. The two brothers drove the cattle back to the meadow at the foot of Mount Olympus, lessening the tedium of the journey with music on the lyre. To the delight of Zeus, they were friends ever after. As a neatherd, Hermes invented another instrument, the rustic pipe (lines 397–512).

Then Apollo said to Hermes, "I am afraid you may steal my lyre and bow,[4] for Zeus has put you in charge of establishing the art of exchange on earth. I won't feel secure until you take a solemn oath." So Hermes swore he would not steal Apollo's property, or go near his house. In return Apollo swore he would consider no friend dearer than Hermes; he also promised to give him a magic wand empowered to execute all the good decrees pronounced by Apollo in his capacity as the

[3] See Appendix B, pages 154–155, on the text of *Hymn*, 473–474.
[4] On the text of line 515, see Appendix B, page 150.

oracular interpreter of the will of Zeus. "But as for this matter of prophecy which you are always referring to,[5] Zeus has ordained that this province must belong to me alone; it is a difficult and responsible position. There is, however, a type of divination which three old witches taught me in my childhood when I was tending cattle on the slopes of Mount Parnassus. Zeus does not think much of it, but you are welcome to it. In addition I put you in charge of the whole animal kingdom, wild and domestic, and you alone shall be messenger to Hades." These favors, the poet goes on to say, show how much Apollo loves Hermes; their friendship was blest by Zeus (lines 513–575). The last few lines of the *Hymn* give a final judgment of the god: Hermes associates with all sorts and conditions of men; he does little good; he spends his whole time playing tricks on mankind (lines 576–580).

The subject of the *Hymn* is Hermes the Thief—in the words of the invocation, "a plunderer, a cattle-raider, a night-watching and door-waylaying thief"— who stole Apollo's cattle on the very day he was born. He is also the Trickster, showing cunning in the execution of his theft, and guile in his verbal exchanges with Apollo and Zeus. His tricks are sometimes magical, as when he transforms himself into a wisp of cloud to pass through the keyhole, or when he makes Apollo's rope of withies take root in the ground. But in the plot of the *Hymn* Hermes the Trickster-Magician fades into the background, and Hermes the Thief occupies the center of the stage.

Hermes is a thief because he appropriates the property of Apollo; the notion of theft in the *Hymn* is firmly based on the recognition of individual property rights. His theft is, moreover, represented as a crime: as such, Apollo refers it to the judgment of Zeus, and Zeus adjudicates in his favor. Property rights are no longer de-

[5] On the text of line 533, see Appendix B, pages 149–150.

rived from the autonomous family but are protected by
a judicial process which enforces the general will of
society as a whole. In terms of this code of justice, Hermes the Thief is a criminal.[6]

Criminal though he is, Hermes has the devotion and
admiration of the author of the *Hymn*. The repetitious
emphasis on Hermes' thievishness in the invocation has
the air of a defiant challenge—*Honi soit qui mal y
pense*. Nowhere is moral disapproval expressed. It is
indeed recognized that thieving does harm to those
who are its victims—in the words of Maia, it is a "nui-
sance"; but of the idea that crime does not pay—in Hesiod's words, that "wrongful gains are baneful gains"—
or of the doctrine of Theognis that it is better to be
poor but honest there is no trace in the *Hymn*.[7] On the
contrary, crime pays Hermes rich dividends. In his *apo-
logia pro vita sua* to his mother, Hermes dismisses her
scruples as childish, and justifies thieving in terms of
the moral philosophy of egoism—"I will take up whatever business is most profitable." His arguments are
left unanswered. Particularly revealing is the poet's
handling of the scene which presents an obvious op-
portunity for vindicating the moral law: the judgment
of Zeus—Zeus who, according to Hesiod, has thrice ten
thousand detectives at work tracking down crime.
Zeus's first reaction is to laugh heartily over his "evil-
minded" son's sophistic oath. As was inevitable, he
orders Hermes to give up the cattle, and Hermes hastens to obey. This attitude of obedience he maintains
for the space of thirteen lines of the *Hymn*. Then he is
up to his old tricks again, preventing Apollo from lead-

[6] See R. J. Bonner and G. Smith, *The Administration of Justice from Homer to Aristotle* (2 vols., Chicago, 1930, 1938), I,
48–51.
[7] Strictly speaking, this is true only of lines 1–512; later in
this chapter it will be shown that lines 513–580 are the work of
a different author, with a different attitude. See *Hymn*, 160;
Hesiod, *Works and Days*, 352; Theognis, 145–146.

ing away the cattle. For the rest, Zeus is only mentioned as being delighted that Hermes and Apollo
finally came to terms.[8]

How are we to explain this tolerant and admiring
attitude toward theft? Since the authorship of the
Hymn is unknown, the problem reduces itself to a defi-
nition in general terms of the type of milieu within
Greek culture to which the author and his audience
can plausibly be assigned, on the ground that in such a
milieu the glorification of Hermes the Thief would be
both appropriate and acceptable. This task is less simple than it is sometimes taken to be. For example, the
standard authorities all regard the *Hymn* as the expression of the uncivilized mores of primitive pastoral life
in backward parts of Greece, such as Arcadia, where
cattle-raiding remained the honorable exploit it was in
the Homeric age.[9] This interpretation rests primarily
on the assumption that, except for the element of
magic, the exploits of the hero are a faithful transcrip-
tion of the mores of the audience for which the *Hymn*
was written. It is indisputable that myths must originally have had some such simple and direct relation to
the behavior of the myth-makers, and no one will dispute the primitive origin of the myth-motifs of the
trickster and the cattle-raider. But it is also true that
myths may be transplanted into an environment different from the one in which they originated and that
they can survive, by subtle adaptation, all manner of
changes in a culture in which they have once taken

[8] *Hymn*, 389–396, 410, 506, 575. Cf. Hesiod, *Works and
Days*, 252–254.
[9] See Radermacher, *Der homerische Hermeshymnus*, 222:
"Ein Kulturdenkmal aus wilderer griechischer Vorzeit, als das
Urbild arkadischer Hirten, die in Bergen und Schluchten einst
ihr Handwerk, halb friedlich und halb ungesittet, trieben."
See also Humbert, *Homère Hymnes*, 104: "Cet Hymne, où une
humanité rustique et naïve cherche à retrouver sa propre image
dans celle du Dieu." Cf. Allen and Halliday, *The Homeric
Hymns*, 269.

root. This truth is ignored by those who regard the
Hymn itself as primitive. They tell us that "the idea of
a trickster-god is one which appeals to the primitive
mind," and forget that the same idea also appeals to
minds that are far from primitive; a case in point is the
medieval epic of Reynard the Fox. Similarly, while it is
true that "the extraordinary feats of a tiny and apparently helpless person is a familiar subject of savage
humor," it is also a popular subject in the folklore of
the American Negro; witness the Brer Rabbit stories,
which, whatever their origin, became the vehicle for
comment on the relations between slave and master.[10]

Actually, we know that the myth of the *Hymn* did
survive the changes which elevated Greek culture
above the primitive level, and survived not merely as a
tradition, but as a living inspiration for new imagina-
tive creations. From the archaic period (the sixth century B.C.)—in which the *Hymn* itself is generally
placed—we have two vase-paintings, one depicting
Apollo demanding the cattle from the baby in the cradle, the other depicting Hermes tucked up in the
cradle with the cattle in the background. The first of
these is from one of the Caeretan Hydriae, a group of
vases famous for the sophisticated sense of humor they
embody, which are ascribed to the most cultured areas
of the Greek world. The second is credited to the Attic
master Brygos. In the same period the equally sophisticated poet Alcaeus wrote a hymn to Hermes, in which
he told of Hermes' theft of the cattle, capped by an
attempt to steal Apollo's bow. In the invocation of this
hymn Alcaeus says, "Hail, thou who rulest over Cyllene: for the spirit moves me to sing of thee"; the spirit
moved him, he was attracted by the subject. The primitive origin of the myth does not prove that the *Hymn*
itself is the product of a primitive environment. There

[10] See R. Benedict, *Encyclopedia of the Social Sciences*, *s.v.*
"Folklore," VI, 288–293.

is no reason why we cannot attribute to the author of
the *Hymn* the same kind of interest in Hermes the
Thief as was shown by Alcaeus, Brygos, and the
painter of the Caeretan Hydria, all of whom belong to
the artistic *avant-garde* of the urban and commercial
culture that was maturing in the most advanced areas
of the Greek world.[11]

The intention of the author is revealed not in the
substance of the myth—traditions which he is not free
to change at will—but in his portrait of Hermes as a
socio-psychological type. The realism of this portrait is
universally acclaimed; it is based on observation, and
hence reveals the sort of environment in which the
Hymn was written and the human type whose patron
and ideal was Hermes the Thief. For although Hermes
is represented as a new-born babe, he is no more a
study in infant psychology than Reynard is a study in
animal psychology. Just as certain qualities attributed
to the fox in medieval folklore made Reynard a good
vehicle for portraying the psychology of the middle
classes under feudalism, so the *Hymn* projects into the
mythical concept of the divine thief an idealized image
of the Greek lower classes, the craftsmen and merchants. Hermes is, as one critic has said, "the little Prometheus." [12] The references to Hermes as an inventor
are frequent, vivid, and elaborate. In all of them the
individual and original genius of the inventor is em-

[11] The Caeretan Hydria is Louvre E702, *Corpus Vasorum
Antiquorum,* France 14, Louvre 9, III.F.a, Plates 8 and 10. The
Caeretan Hydriae are regarded as having been produced in
either Ionia or southern Italy about the middle of the sixth
century; see E. Pottier, "Fragments d'une Hydrie de Caere," in
Fondation E. Piot, *Monuments et Mémoires,* 33(1933):67–94.
On the Brygos vase see J. D. Beazley, *Attic Red-Figure Vase-
Painters* (Oxford, 1942), p. 246, no. 6. On Alcaeus, Frg. 2
(Diehl), see Bowra, *Greek Lyric Poetry,* 174–175; Wilamo-
witz, *Sappho und Simonides,* 311–312; and Wunsch, in Pauly-
Wissowa, *s.v.* "Hymnus," IX.145.

[12] Schmid-Stählin, *Geschichte der griechischen Literatur,* Part
I, Vol. I, p. 237.

phasized; this is the typical conceit of the Attic craftsmen, as displayed in the proud signatures of the potters. The praise of the lyre—"This is marvelous music
that I hear now for the first time"—compares with the
exultant vase-inscription, "Euphronius never equaled
this." [13] In the description of the invention of the sandals Hermes' skill at improvisation is emphasized; improvisation is the talent in which Themistocles, the
genius of the industrial and mercantile party, excelled
all, according to Thucydides.[14] From the observation of
craftsmen at work are derived such vivid touches of
psychological portraiture as Hermes' joyous laughter,
his "eureka" when he gets the idea of the tortoise-shell
lyre.[15] In three different passages the *Hymn* mentions
the sparkle in Hermes' bright eyes, the first time when
Hermes is making the lyre: it is the gleam in the eyes
of a craftsman enjoying his work.[16] The craftsman also
suggested the idea of the bustle that constantly sur-
rounds the activities of Hermes, "who, as soon as he
had issued from his mother's womb, did not long remain lying in the sacred cradle, but up he jumped and
went hunting for the cattle of Apollo"; the lyre was
constructed "no sooner said than done"; while he is
playing it "new plans occupy his mind"; in his hercu-
lean labors to prepare two of the cattle for sacrifice,
"work piled on work." [17]

And it is not only Hermes' technical ability and his
delight in technique that are modeled on the craftsman
type, but also his moral philosophy, and even his manners. Hermes expounds his creed in his speech to his
mother: he tells her that her scruples about his activi-

[13] *Hymn*, 25–51, 76–86, 107–111, 222–226, 346–349, 443–
455, 482–488, 511.
[14] *Hymn*, 86; Thucydides, I.138.
[15] *Hymn*, 29–38; cf. Schmid-Stählin, *loc. cit.*
[16] *Hymn*, 45–46, 278, 415.
[17] *Hymn*, 20–22, 46, 62, 120. Note the parody of Hesiod,
Works and Days, 382.

ties are childish; that he intends to put his own interests first, and follow the career with the most profit in
it; that a life of affluence and luxury would be better
than living in a dreary cave; that he is determined to
get equality with Apollo—by illegal means if he cannot
get it by legal means (that is, by gift of Zeus): he will
go so far as to break into Apollo's Delphic treasury.
What is this if not the businessman's creed, the philosophy of the acquisitive way of life which the Greek
philosophers of the fifth century discuss; to use a
phrase coined in the archaic age, what is it if not the
doctrine that "money is the man?" [18] This philosophy
inspires not only Hermes' theft, but also his inventions.
In his first speech, addressed to the tortoise, the idea of
the profit that can be got from the tortoise is repeated
three times; Hermes is particularly pleased over being
the pioneer in the business—"I will be the first to get
profit from you," he says. He makes a mocking allusion
to the traditional and rustic use of the tortoise as a
charm—"While you live you will be a good charm, if
you die you will become a pretty singer"—and then he
proceeds to kill her. Most pointed of all is the delight-
ful parody of the line in Hesiod already quoted as an
epitome of Hesiod's rejection of the new commercial
culture; Hermes applies it to the tortoise, in the same
way as the spider might apply it to the fly, "You come
along with me; it is better to stay at home since the
outside world is noxious." Such sophistication in the art
of parody is a significant indication of the type of audience for which the *Hymn* was composed; even more
significant is the selection of the passage to be parodied
—a maxim expressing Hesiod's rejection of the new
commercial culture.[19]

And then there are Hermes' manners and morals in

18 *Hymn*, 163–181; cf. Pindar, *Isthmian*, II.11; Alcaeus, Frg.
101 (Diehl); Pauly-Wissowa, *s.v.* "Aristodemus," II.920–921.
19 *Hymn*, 30–38; Hesiod, *Works and Days*, 365.

the more personal sense. They are on the vulgar side.
For his first song on the lyre he selects a subject which
a critic delicately refers to as unhomeric. Shelley translates:

> He sung how Jove and May of the bright sandal
>   Dallied in love not quite legitimate;
> And his own birth, still scoffing at the scandal,
>   And naming his own name, did celebrate.

He is litigious, skillful at making the worse appear the
better reason. He lies brazenly to Apollo. He tries a
mixture of trickery, bluffing, flattery, and cajoling to
persuade Apollo to let him keep the cattle, and it suc-
ceeds. These are the essential traits of the impudent
and smooth-talking self-seeker that haunted the Athenian agora, portrayed by Aristophanes in the Sausage-
Seller of the *Knights*, the Unjust Reason of the *Clouds*,
and the litigious type satirized in the *Wasps*. And as for
Hermes' shameless omen, the "unfortunate servant of
the belly," where do the commentators turn for analo-
gies except to Aristophanes? [20] Although the type is best
portrayed by Aristophanes, it is also found in the archaic period. Already Hesiod has his brother Perses
typed as a man who hangs around the agora and prefers to make money dishonestly, particularly by legal
chicanery. But the best example is the sixth-century Ionian poet Hipponax, of whom a critic says, "The moral-
istic anthologists found little of value in his poems. He
hardly ever rises above the level of his own personal
squabbles and needs, and stories from the lowest type

[20] *Hymn*, 57–59, 296–297, 312, 367–386; Schmid-Stählin, *loc.
cit.* Cf. Eitrem, "Der homerische Hymnus an Hermes," *Philologus*, 65(1906):274: "Er [Hermes] verwendet dabei alle die
Kniffe, an die man in den athenischen Gerichtshöfen gewohnt
war." Radermacher (*op. cit.*, 216) points out the similarity to
the Aristophanic type of the βωμολόχος and ἀλαζών. How he
reconciles this with his view of the *Hymn* as "ein Kulturdenkmal
aus wilderer griechischer Vorzeit" is a question he leaves unanswered.

of everyday experience. In general his topics are personal abuse, threats, complaints, direct begging—for
warm clothes and shoes, food, money. This gentleman,
the last word in realism, individualism, and vulgarity,
found even the simple iamb of Archilochus too exalted
for his purposes." Hipponax, significantly enough,
found Hermes the most congenial god; he is in fact the
only personality in Greek literature of whom it may be
said that he walked with Hermes all the days of his
life. Hermes in the *Hymn* is an idealized Hipponax.[21]

The portrait of Hermes as the ideal of the new commercial culture is projected into the traditional concepts of Hermes the Trickster and Thief. Sometimes
the *Hymn* relates Hermes the Trickster to Hermes the
Craftsman by preserving the original notion of
trickery as magic skill: the sandals are described as the
work of a mighty demon; the lyre, which is generally
personified, is represented as a miraculous creation;
Apollo's rope of withies magically takes root in the
ground "due to the will of Hermes the stealthy-
minded." [22] In general, however, Hermes' trickery symbolizes the self-interested cunning that is characteristic
of Aristophanes' agora type. His speech to Maia, his
lying denial to Apollo, his speech before the judgment
seat of Zeus, and his speech to Apollo in the negotiations leading up to the exchange are all described as
"cunning." In his speech to Maia he is not trying to
trick her; what is "cunning" is the acquisitive philosophy expressed in the speech. In his denial to Apollo
and his speech to Zeus he is cunning in the use of
courtroom sophistry. In the negotiations with Apollo
he shows shrewdness in bargaining.[23]

Not only as trickster, but also as thief Hermes sym-

[21] Hesiod, *Works and Days*, 28–29; Hipponax, Frgs. 4, 24a,
26, 27, 37 (Diehl); Schmid-Stählin, *op. cit.*, 400 (translated).
[22] *Hymn*, 343, 413, 440–455.
[23] *Hymn*, 162, 260, 317, 387, 463.

bolizes the new commercial culture. In his speech to
Maia, which, as one commentator has said, contains
the gist of the whole *Hymn,* Hermes deduces his justification of a career of theft from the ethical principles
of acquisitive individualism—the duty of self-help and
the doctrine that money is the man. An even more obvious clue to the meaning of the *Hymn* is contained in
the reason advanced by Apollo for demanding that
Hermes swear an oath not to steal his property—"Son
of Maia, messenger full of shifty guile, I am afraid that
you may steal from me both my lyre and my curved
bow; for you have received from Zeus the office of establishing the practice of commerce among mankind."
Apollo explicitly identifies commerce with theft.[24]

This equation of commerce with theft has been compared to the attacks on the profit motive in some modern economic theories. Whether or not the comparison
is justified, the point of view expressed in the *Hymn* is
virtually axiomatic in Greek moral philosophy. Every-
one is familiar with the aristocratic prejudice against
retail trade and manual labor, rationalized by Plato
into the ethical doctrine that all professions in which
the end is profit are vulgar and incompatible with the
pursuit of virtue. The prejudice is ultimately derived
from the conflict between the traditional patriarchal

[24] *Hymn,* 514–517. The point is entirely missed by the modern
commentators: Allen and Halliday, *op. cit.,* 342; Radermacher,
op. cit., 162–163; Eitrem, *op. cit.,* 278; Robert, "Zum homerischen Hermeshymnos," *Hermes,* 41(1906):413–414. They all
take "practice of commerce" or "acts of exchange" to be an
euphemism for stealing itself, thus giving the sense "since Zeus
placed you in charge of stealing, I am afraid lest you steal my
bow and lyre." Note that the *Hymn* makes clear that the stealing of which Hermes is the patron is an urban as well as a rural
phenomenon. In line 15 Hermes is called a "door-waylaying
thief"—a reference to the practice described in Aristophanes'
Birds, 496–497: "I just stuck my head outside the wall and a
bandit clubbed me in the back." In line 283 Apollo prophesies
that Hermes will often "bore into rich men's houses"; theft by
wall-boring is frequently alluded to by Aristophanes and the
Attic Orators.

morality, sustained by the aristocracy, and the new
economy of acquisitive individualism—the conflict of
Metis and Themis in Hesiod. One of the results of this
attitude was to identify trade with cheating, and the
pursuit of profit with theft. As we saw in the preceding
chapter, Hesiod regards acquisitive individualism as
"theft" and "robbery." Solon uses the same terminology
in his indictment of those who pursue wealth without
regard to the common weal: "The very citizens, in
their folly, are willing to contribute to the destruction
of our great city, yielding to the temptation of riches.
They do not have the sense to set limits to their super-
abundance. They grow rich through yielding to the
temptation of unjust practices, and sparing neither sacred nor public property, they go stealing and robbing
wherever they can." In Aristophanes' *Plutus,* when
Poverty argues that "Good manners dwell with me,
while insolence goes with Wealth," Chremyles an-
swers, satirizing the enlightened ethics of mercantile
Athens, "It is perfectly good manners here to steal and
bore walls." Theft by wall-boring, of which Apollo ac-
cuses Hermes in the *Hymn,* is used metaphorically by
Demosthenes to mean sharp practice in commerce;
Plato argues that wall-boring is only a bolder expression of the same love of wealth which animates the
merchant and the craftsman. Socrates in the *Gorgias*
describes the "life of desire" (a more abstract expression for the acquisitive way of life) as the "life of
a robber." [25]

Hesiod, Solon, and Plato all use "theft" and "robbery" as interchangeable metaphors in their denuncia-
tions of acquisitive individualism, thus ignoring the
distinction between forcible and fraudulent appropria-

[25] See Glotz, *Ancient Greece at Work,* 160–162; H. Francotte,
L'Industrie dans la Grèce ancienne (Brussels, 1900), I, 246–253;
Solon, Frg. 3 (Diehl); Aristophanes, *Plutus,* 565; Demosthenes,
XXXV.9; Plato, *Laws,* 831E, and *Gorgias,* 507E. On Hesiod, see
above, Chapter IV, notes 10 and 11.

tion. The *Hymn* also ignores the distinction, by attributing a cattle-raid to Hermes the Thief, and by describing him as a "robber" and "plunderer." The mythical
symbol for acquisitive individualism is thus composed
of exactly the same ingredients as the verbal symbol.
This coalescence of the notions of theft and robbery is
due not to an obliteration of the distinction between
force and fraud, but to the fact that robbery has ceased
to be the honorable exploit it was in the Homeric age,
and has come to be regarded, along with theft, as a
crime. Hesiod calls robbery "wrongful," and specifically condemns cattle-raiding: "Not an ox would be
lost, if there were no wicked neighbors." By the time
of Hesiod the kings had ceased to be the leaders of ma-
rauding bands; they now formed a landed aristocracy
which had a vested interest in the suppression of all
attacks on property, including both robbery and theft.
This change of heart is reflected in Hesiod's *Shield of
Heracles,* in which Heracles, one of the great cattle-
raiders of Greek mythology, is represented as a re-
formed character now applying his prowess to the task
of ridding the earth of such nuisances as Cycnus, who
"lay in wait for the hecatombs on the way to Pytho and
robbed them by force." At the same time that Heracles
renounces cattle-raiding, Hermes takes it up. Combined with theft, Hermes' robbery completes the mythical symbol of the pursuit of wealth without regard to
the dictates of justice and Themis.[26]

In society which shares Benjamin Franklin's opinion
that commerce is generally cheating, the merchant is a
thief whatever he does; it is only natural for him to

[26] Hesiod, *Works and Days,* 356, 348; *Shield of Heracles,*
480. Hermes first appears as cattle-raider in a poem of the
Hesiodic school (Hesiod, Frg. 153, ed. Rzach), which may be as
late as the sixth century B.C.; cf. Schmid-Stählin, *op. cit.,* Part I,
Vol. I, pp. 268–269. This poem first launched the myth which is
told in the *Hymn.* On the relation between the two, see Appendix A.

react by justifying and idealizing theft. In the Middle
Ages the Church's doctrine on usury confronted the
merchant with the same dilemma: as one wit said, if
you practice usury you end up in hell, and if you don't
you end up in destitution. The medieval merchant accepted his own equation with the thief: he carried a
thief's thumb as a talisman to help him in his business,
shared his patron Saint Nicholas with the thief, and
made Reynard the Fox his hero and ideal.[27] In Greece
the philosophic defenders of individualism, lacking the
doctrine that

> Thus God and Nature formed the general frame,
> And bade self-love and social be the same,

proclaimed the war of every man against every man,
and attempted to justify what Socrates called the life
of a robber. The average tradesman found his self-
justification in Hermes. Thus fortified, the impudent
Sausage-Seller in Aristophanes' Knights not only admits that he steals, but wants to perjure himself by
Hermes of the Agora to prove that he steals.[28]

[27] "Qui facit usuram, vadit ad infernum; qui non facit, vadit
ad inopiam," quoted by R. H. Tawney in his Religion and the
Rise of Capitalism (New York, 1926), 11. Cf. Bächtold-Stäubli,
Handwörterbuch des deutschen Aberglaubens, s.v. "Nikolaus,"
VI, 1088–1089, and "Dieb, Diebstahl," II, 239–240; R. Benedict,
Encyclopedia of the Social Sciences, s.v. "Folklore," VI, 292.

[28] Aristophanes, Knights, 296–298. Diodorus (V.75) says
Hermes invented "measures and weights and commercial profits
and how to appropriate other people's property by stealth."
Plato (Cratylus, 407E) says Hermes symbolizes "theft and verbal deceit and the ethics of the agora." See also T. Zielinski,
The Religion of Ancient Greece (Oxford, 1926), 53: "Among the
ancients, as in our own time, trade was of two sorts: wholesale
import and export trade (emporike) and local retail trade
(kapelike); the first enjoyed much respect, the second very little.
The fact that Hermes extended his protection even over the
second, with its inherent knavery, could not help lowering the
significance of the god himself." Zielinski shares the Greek attitude toward trade; hence he urges us (ibid., 115) to "forget as
completely as may be" Hermes the god of thieves, and concen-
trate on Hermes the god of international law, etc., calling these

The connection with commerce and craftsmanship persists throughout the various stages of the mythology of Hermes; and the *Hymn*, despite superficial appearances, is no exception. At the same time the *Hymn* grafts new themes onto the parent stem of the myth—themes derived from experience, which give the myth new life by renewing its contact with the ever-changing reality it symbolizes. In addition to its novel portrait of Hermes' personality, the *Hymn* contains two new themes which radically alter the meaning of the myth—the theme of strife between Hermes and Apollo, and the representation of Hermes as a newborn baby.

The responsibility for the strife between Hermes and Apollo falls on Hermes: he is clearly the aggressor. His ambitious aggressiveness is the mainspring of the whole plot of the *Hymn*. As he explains to his mother, ambition was his motive for stealing the cattle. His determination to hold what he has makes him prevent Apollo from leading away the cattle, the episode which leads to the revelation of the lyre and the subsequent exchange. It is Hermes' aggressiveness that makes Apollo feel insecure even after the exchange and leads him to extract a further oath from Hermes and make further concessions to him. This trait in Hermes' character is in sharp contrast with Homer's picture of Hermes the loyal subordinate of Zeus.[29]

The goal of Hermes' ambition is equality with

---

other aspects alone expressions of "genuine religion." Quite apart from the fact that these aspects were all interconnected (see above, Chapter I), this hypostatization of selected phenomena as "genuine religion" is entirely subjective and sacrifices the facts to a sentimental urge to assimilate Greek to modern religious values. A Hermes without the Thief is a chimerical abstraction. In contrast with Pope's dictum quoted in the text, the orthodox Greek attitude is stated by Euripides (*Phoenissae*, 395): "We are slaves of profit contrary to the laws of nature."

[29] Cf. Radermacher, *op. cit.*, 217–218; *Odyssey*, 5.103–104.

Apollo. It is the cattle of Apollo that Hermes chooses to steal, though all the gods have herds and all the cattle of the gods are grazing together when Hermes separates fifty of them belonging to Apollo. Hermes and Apollo are contrasting figures in Greek mythology; the poet exploits this contrast, particularly when he brings the two gods together for the first time. Apollo is a majestic figure as he approaches Hermes' home, "his ample shoulders curtained in a purple cloud." When this majestic figure, "far-darting Apollo in person," appears, Hermes makes himself as small as possible. But Apollo cannot be deceived: "The son of Leto knew, and did not fail to know, the nymph and her son." This is the formula which Hesiod uses when Zeus unmasks Prometheus: "Zeus, whose mind is full of immortal wisdom, knew and did not fail to know the trick." With the power as well as the knowledge of Zeus, Apollo threatens to hurl the infant to the depths of Hell—the same threat is used in the *Iliad* when Zeus delivers a speech to the rebellious gods. This is the familiar contrast between Power and Helplessness, as in the Brer Rabbit stories; there is in it the same invitation to the reader's sympathies which Hermes addresses to Zeus— "Uphold the cause of the young and helpless." [30]

Hermes' ambition is to secure the "status" and "privileges" that will place him on a par with Apollo, the aristocrat of Olympus. The result is not merely strife, in the sense in which Hesiod uses the term to designate competitive individualism; it is "civil war within the community of kindred," to use a phrase of Solon's. The theme of strife between Hermes and Apollo translates into mythical language the insurgence of the Greek lower classes and their demands for equality with the aristocracy. The *Hymn* thus reflects the social crisis of the archaic age—the crisis depicted by Solon when he

[30] *Hymn*, 217, 234, 237–240, 243, 256, 386. Cf. Boettcher, *De Hymno in Mercurium*, 16, 21, 96, 98, 105, 107.

says that the unrestrained pursuit of wealth has brought Athens to the verge of "civil war within the community of kindred," and by Theognis when he says that no city remains long at peace "when this becomes the aim of evil men, individual profits at the expense of the common weal; thence come civil wars and the shedding of kindred blood and tyrannies." It is the crisis that Solon attempted to solve by a redistribution of "status" and "privilege": "To the common people I have given a sufficient amount of privilege, not taking away from their status, nor adding to it superfluously." Theognis laments that a similar solution was applied in his home city of Megara: "Our city is still a city, but the folk are not the same. Those who before knew nothing of judgments or laws, but rubbed their ribs bare with the goat-skins they used for clothing and stayed outside the city like wild deer, now they are the nobility, and those who were noble before, now they are nobodies. Who can endure this sight?" If Hermes is "the little Prometheus," then the *Hymn* brings us to a period not far distant from the release of that Prometheus whom Hesiod left bound in adamantine chains.[31]

[31] *Hymn*, 172 (τιμή), and 291 (γέρας); Solon, Frgs. 3 and 5 (Diehl); Theognis, 47–52, 63–68. Hermes seeks ἰσοτιμία; cf. Apollo ἰσότιμος, i.e., sharing equality with Zeus (W. Dittenberger, *Orientis Graeciae Inscriptiones Selectae* [Leipzig, 1903–05], 234, line 25). Compare the political struggle for ἰσονομία, Herodotus, III.80, 142, and V.37. On the parallelism between the heavenly and the earthly dispensation (διανομαί), see Hirzel, *Themis, Dike und Verwandtes,* 246. On the social struggle of the archaic age, see W. K. Prentice, "The Fall of Aristocracies and the Emancipation of Men's Minds," *Transactions and Proceedings of the American Philological Association,* 56(1925):162–171, and A. A. Trever, "Economic and Social Conditions in Megara," *Classical Philology,* 20(1925):115–132. Cf. Schmid-Stählin, *op. cit.,* Part I, Vol. I, p. 237: "Das Emporstreben der niederen intelligenten Schichten ist in Hermes verkörpert." On Hesiod's myth of Prometheus, see *ibid.,* 247. On Apollo as the aristocratic god, see S. Smertenko, "The Political Relations of the Delphic Oracle," *Studies in Greek Religion* (*University of Oregon Studies, Humanistic Series,* Vol. 5, no. 1 (1935).

The drama of the contemporary social scene is also infused into the representation of Hermes as a baby. By this device the poet accentuates the contrast between Power and Helplessness, between the established authority of the aristocracy and the native intelligence of the rising lower classes; as in the Brer Rabbit stories, our sympathies are enlisted on the side of the underdog. Furthermore, the baby Hermes "makes good" on the very day of his birth. To emphasize Hermes' meteoric rise in status the poet exploits the widespread theme of the marvelous child who proves his divinity by precocious prodigies. It is the symbol of the birth of a new world in which, as a result of the redistribution of status described by Solon and Theognis, the lower classes come into their own. Hermes is the Pantagruel of the Greek Renaissance.[32]

Did Hermes get that equality with Apollo which was his ambition? This question is answered in the exchange scene. Hermes gave Apollo the lyre, and Apollo gave Hermes the neatherd's staff. Most critics feel that Hermes got the worst of the bargain. Hermes, they say, forfeits his marvelous invention, and Apollo passes on

[32] On the theme of the marvelous child, see Allen and Halliday, *op. cit.*, 269; Radermacher, *op. cit.*, 64, 197. Radermacher interpreted the form of the myth in the *Hymn* as reflecting a situation in which the cult of Hermes was actually a new arrival intruding into an area previously monopolized by the cult of Apollo. This hypothesis is altogether improbable for any part of the Greek world even in the seventh century B.C.: those who stratify the Greek Pantheon into different chronological strata put Hermes in the oldest, and Apollo in the latest, stratum. Hence Wilamowitz (*Glaube der Hellenen*, I, 328) reversed the interpretation of the *Hymn*, maintaining that Apollo is intruding into an area previously monopolized by Hermes. In this, as in many other cases in Greek mythology, the effort to explain the myth in terms of cult-diffusion yields contradictory results and should be abandoned. Both interpretations neglect the possibility of a conflict between two already established cults (see below, pp. 93–105). A rise in the status of one cult at the expense of the other is sufficient to explain the form of the myth in the *Hymn*.

to Hermes the menial task of tending cattle.[33] Strangely enough, however, neither the poet nor Hermes seems to regard the exchange as a setback for Hermes. The initiative throughout the exchange scene is in his hands. When Apollo is about to lead the cattle away, Hermes "freezes" them. It is Hermes who produces the lyre, and shows it off to Apollo like a merchant in a bazaar. Apollo is swept off his feet; in the first flush of his enthusiasm he says the lyre is worth fifty oxen, the number Hermes had stolen; he apparently thinks that to exchange the lyre for oxen would be not a bad bargain for Hermes but a real tribute to the value of his invention. His actual offer, however, is considerably toned down—he only makes vague promises of "wealth and honor." In his reply Hermes proposes the terms on which the bargain was actually struck and the speech is described as a sample of Hermes' shrewdness in bargaining. After flowery compliments to Apollo and praise of the lyre he ignores the vague offer of wealth and honor and asks specifically for what he got, charge over the cattle. Hermes knows what he wants and gets what he wants.[34]

If the lyre is worth fifty oxen, Hermes, in losing the lyre and gaining the oxen, comes out even in cash value—no great achievement for the genius of theft and trickery—and Apollo comes out ahead in social prestige. Was this the goal of Hermes' ambition? The truth is that the terms of the bargain have been misunderstood. Hermes does not lose the lyre, Apollo does not lose the cattle; they agree to share both lyre and cattle. Each initiates the other into his own art. The

[33] The best exposition of this interpretation is by Schmid and Stählin (op. cit., Part I, Vol. I, pp. 237–238).

[34] Hymn, 405–512. In the interpretation of lines 409–413 I follow Allen and Halliday (op. cit., 330–332) as against Radermacher (op. cit., 145–146). On lines 414–416 Allen and Halliday are to be preferred to Radermacher, though I believe the lacuna which they both accept can be avoided; see Appendix B.

poet does not define the nature of the exchange explicitly because his audience knew that both Hermes and
Apollo were in fact patrons of both the musical and the
pastoral worlds; indirectly, however, his narrative
points to the correct interpretation. Thus in his final
speech Hermes lectures Apollo on the use of the lyre,
as a teacher would a pupil; while willing to share the
patent, he takes pains to point out that he remains the
inventor—"I am not stingy about your learning *my* art
. . . . Just as Zeus has initiated you into his oracular
secrets, so I will initiate you into *my* new art. . . .
Enjoy the lyre, receiving it from *my* hands; only let
the glory be *mine*." Apollo for his part subsequently
refers to the lyre as a "token" of friendship between
him and Hermes; he is referring to the custom of seal-
ing an agreement by breaking a token and giving each
party half of it. As for the cattle, what Hermes actually
says is this: "I will give you the lyre; in return let *us*
herd the cattle. Then the cows will mingle with the
bulls and breed sufficiently." Hermes did not steal
Apollo's whole herd, but only fifty cows, leaving the
bull; he envisages a union of the fifty cows with the
rest of Apollo's herd, which at no point is involved in
the exchange. Finally the poet says: "They *both* turned
the cattle to the meadow, and went back to Olympus,
both amusing themselves with the lyre." Hermes has
every right to be content with the exchange; he has
achieved exact equality with Apollo.[35]

[35] *Hymn*, 465, 471–474, 476–477, 491–494, 503–506, 527. On
the text of lines 471–474 and 503, see Appendix B. On the
meaning of line 477, see Humbert, *op. cit.*, 135; Radermacher
(*op. cit.*, 156) translates it "give me a gift in return"; but
Hermes does not come to the *quid pro quo* until line 491. The
exchange is correctly interpreted by Kuiper ("De discrepantiis
Hymni Homerici in Mercurium," *Mnemosyne*, n.s., 38[1910]:
47): "Quae si uno tenore perlegas, constabit opinor tibi, poetae
hoc fuisse propositum, ut jura Mercurii Apollinis honoribus
aequata hac arte illustraret." Allen and Halliday (*op. cit.*, 340)
and Radermacher (*op. cit.*, 160) say that Hermes *consoled* him-

What does the poet mean by attributing to Hermes equality with Apollo? Hermes and Apollo are symbols of rival forces in the social and political conflict of the archaic age; the myth credits the lower classes with having achieved the equality they fought for. But Hermes and Apollo are not symbols invented by the poet; he is writing about two recognized Greek cults. His mythical description of the relations between Hermes and Apollo is not only an interpretation of the social scene but also an interpretation of the relations between the two cults.

From the *Hymn* and other sources we know that there were many points of contact between the cults of Hermes and Apollo. Both were gods of music and of divination; both were patrons of youth, and hence of athletics; both were guardians of the house and of roads; both were patrons of the pastoral life. These are the facts which the poet is explaining. What is his explanation? "The close friendship between Hermes and Apollo," the modern editors answer, pointing to the poet's statement that the two gods were friends ever after.[36] It is easy to read too much into this statement. To enter a state of "friendship" may mean only that open hostilities have been concluded: in the *Iliad*, when two warriors, tired of combat, agree to meet again on another day, this agreement is called a "friendship." And it is not without significance that after Hermes and Apollo have become "friends," the

---

self for the loss of the lyre by inventing the pipe; there is no justification for this interpretation in the text, which says merely, "And then he devised another invention" (line 511). The *Hymn* represents the lyre as the joint property of Hermes and Apollo, just as Pindar (*Pythian*, I.2) represents it to be the joint property of Apollo and the Muses.

[36] Farnell, *Cults*, V, 29: "He [Hermes] may have also become especially interested in the ephebi from his close friendship with Apollo"; cf. Preller-Robert, I, 393, and Wernicke in Pauly-Wissowa, *s.v.* "Apollo," II.37. Cf. *Hymn*, 506–508, 574–575.

quarrel breaks out anew, ending in the formation of a
second "friendship." Even if the poet predicts harmonious relations between the two gods after the final settlement, the settlement itself is the climax of a contest
in wit and strength. The ownership of the various
properties in dispute carries with it recognition as the
patron god of a particular sphere of human activity.
Hermes' inroads into Apollo's property imply that the
cult of Hermes was actually making inroads into
spheres hitherto presided over by Apollo; Hermes himself tells his mother that his ambition is to establish
himself as a god with the same holy attributes as
Apollo. The *Hymn* takes the points of contact between
Hermes and Apollo as reflecting not cooperation but
competition between the two cults.[37]

The poet discusses in greatest detail the relation between Hermes and Apollo as patrons of music—his
own art. The burden of his discussion is that Hermes is
competent in every type of music associated with
Apollo, and is even Apollo's superior. For his first song
on the lyre Hermes chooses a subject "such as young
revellers sing at banquets, matching their wits in alternate sallies." When Apollo hears the lyre, he says that
in all his experience of clever songs by young men at
banquets he had never heard such effective music.
Apollo and Hermes are thus represented as rival patrons of symposiastic music, and Hermes' new invention is said to be superior to anything previously
known to Apollo.[38] Nor is Hermes' skill confined to
light music. To show off the lyre to Apollo he sang "of
the immortal gods and the dark earth, how they were
born and how each received its portion"; his subject is
a theogony—which is likewise the subject of Apollo's

[37] *Iliad*, 7.302; cf. Glotz, *Solidarité de la famille*, 140–141;
Hymn, 172–173.
[38] *Hymn*, 55–56, 454; note also that Hermes is called "companion of the banquet" in line 436. For this type of symposiastic
music, see Pindar, *Olympian*, I.15–17, and Herodotus, VI.129.

first song in the *Hymn to Apollo,* a poem with which
our author is fully familiar.[39]

The poet does not merely represent Hermes and
Apollo as rival musical gods; he takes sides in the controversy. He shows his own sympathies by putting into
Hermes' mouth a speech on "the artist in relation to his
instrument," just as it is Apollo who lectures on "the
nature of prophecy." [40] When two cults are in competition, mythology becomes a vehicle for propaganda. In
attributing the invention of the tortoise-shell lyre to
Hermes, the poet is already indulging in propaganda.
The facts are, as is implied by the exchange scene, that
both Hermes and Apollo were regarded as patrons of
the tortoise-shell lyre; some preferred Hermes, and
some Apollo, and each side expressed its preference by
attributing the invention of the instrument to its favorite.[41] The poet goes further; to the greater glory of
Hermes, he denies Apollo musical attributes universally regarded to be his. Apollo's usual musical instrument was the cithara, a stringed instrument similar to
the tortoise-shell lyre, but made of wood. The poet,
though perfectly familiar with the very frequent repre-

[39] *Hymn,* 427–428; *Homeric Hymn to Apollo,* 190–191. Hesiod places his *Theogony* under the patronage of Apollo and the
Muses; see lines 94–95. On our author's familiarity with both
Hesiod and the *Hymn to Apollo,* see Boettcher, *De Hymno in
Mercurium,* 96–109, and Dornseiff, "Zum homerischen Hermeshymnos," *Rheinisches Museum,* N. F. 87(1938):80–84. This
is the refutation of the argument that Hermes has cheapened the
lyre by using it for unhomeric subjects, and hence has to forfeit
it, in the exchange scene, to Apollo the true artist; Schmid-
Stählin, *op. cit.,* Part I, Vol. I, pp. 237–238.

[40] *Hymn,* 482–488, 540–549. Cf. Radermacher, *op. cit.,* 157:
"Jetzt spricht nicht mehr Hermes, jetzt spricht der Dichter
selbst von einer ihm vertrauten Kunst."

[41] The invention of the lyre is attributed to Apollo by Plato
(*Republic,* 399D–E), Callimachus (*Hymn to Delos,* 253),
Diodorus (V.75), and Plutarch (*De Musica,* 14, 1136A). These
are all writers with conservative or aristocratic sympathies. Pindar (*Pythian,* V.65) attributes to Apollo the invention of the
citharis, by which he probably means string-music, including
both the cithara and the lyre.

sentations in early art and literature of Apollo playing
the cithara while the Muses dance, makes out Hermes'
invention to be the first stringed instrument of any
kind, putting into Apollo's mouth the statement that it
was the flute that he had played in the circle of the
Muses.[42] In the same spirit the poet advances a claim,
unique in Greek literature, that Hermes, not Apollo, is
the companion of the Muses. When Hermes sings his
theogony, he sings "first of Mnemosyne, Mother of the
Muses, for she drew the son of Maia as her lot." Apollo
naturally hastens to answer, "I, too, am a companion of
the Muses." The rivalry breaks out into claim and
counter-claim. Mnemosyne "drew the son of Maia as
her lot," a phrase which means that Hermes is the *consort* of Mnemosyne. An earlier tradition made Apollo
the father of three of Mnemosyne's daughters, the
Muses; the poet is claiming for Hermes an honor previously accorded to Apollo.[43]

The *Hymn* not only asserts the existence of rivalry
between the cults of Hermes and Apollo in consequence of the intrusion of Hermes into spheres previously reserved for Apollo, but also, as a propagandistic
effort on behalf of Hermes, is itself testimony to the
truth of its assertion. This idea that the two cults were
in conflict has not been taken seriously by modern his-

[42] Hymn, 452; cf. Allen and Halliday, 335. Literary references
to Apollo playing the cithara include: *Iliad,* 1.603; *Odyssey,*
8.488; Hesiod, *Shield of Heracles,* 201–203. For illustrations in
archaic art, see Farnell, *Cults,* IV, 325–326, and J. Overbeck,
Griechische Kunstmythologie, Vol. III, Book V, pp. 41–62.

[43] *Hymn,* 429–430, 450. The meaning of line 430 is missed
by Humbert (*op. cit.,* 133), Radermacher (*op. cit.,* 149–150),
and Allen and Halliday (*op. cit.,* 334). For λάχε in this sense,
compare the Latin *consors* and Pindar, *Pythian,* II.27; also
Sophocles, *Antigone,* 917–918, 1240–1241. For Apollo as the
companion of the Muses, see *Iliad,* 1.603–604; Hesiod, *Theogony,* 94; *Homeric Hymn to Apollo,* 189; Alcman, Frg. 34
(Diehl); and Pausanias, V.18.4 (the chest of Kypselus). Apollo
is said to be the father of three Muses by Eumelus (Frg. 17,
Epicorum Graecorum Fragmenta, ed. G. Kinkel).

torians of Greek religion, many of whom seem to treat
Greek religion as if it were a coherent system of
dogma. They seek to establish a harmonious division of
labor between Hermes and Apollo within the musical
sphere: some say that Hermes is the god of simple rustic music, Apollo the god of the more advanced forms;
others that Hermes is the lyre-maker, Apollo the lyre-
artist; still others that Hermes is the patron of the lyre,
Apollo of the cithara.[44] The variety of solutions in itself suggests that the whole approach is a mistaken
one. This tendency to reduce the dynamic contradictions of Greek mythology in its vital period to a dull,
flat consistency dates back as far as the learned Hellenistic mythographers. Their tortuous efforts to harmo-
nize prove that harmony cannot be achieved—for
example, Diodorus' theory that although Hermes did
invent the lyre, the invention was merely a rediscovery
of an instrument formerly belonging to Apollo but de-
stroyed by him in a fit of remorse over his cruel punish-
ment of Marsyas, who had dared to set himself up as
Apollo's rival in music.[45] The theory that Hermes was
solely the god of rustic music breaks down in the light
of Hermes' association with the tortoise-shell lyre,
which in function belonged to the cultured pleasures of
urban life, and in origin to the new civilization pioneered by the commercial cities of Ionia in the archaic
age.[46] The theory that Hermes was the lyre-maker is

[44] Wilamowitz, *Glaube der Hellenen*, I, 168; Roscher, *Lexikon
der Mythologie*, I, 2373; Farnell, *Cults*, V, 27; Schmid-Stählin,
op. cit., Part I, Vol. I, p. 238; Allen and Halliday, *op. cit.*, 270.

[45] Diodorus, V.75. For Hermes the inventor, Apollo the artist,
see Diodorus III.59. For Hermes and the lyre, Apollo and the
cithara, see Bion, Frg. VI.8 (ed. Wilamowitz), and Pausanias,
V.14.8.

[46] The instrument described in the *Hymn* has two peculiarities: it is made from tortoise shell, and it has seven strings. On
the history of the lyre see Abert, in Pauly-Wissowa, XIII.2479–
2489. On the difference in construction between the lyre and
the cithara, see M. Guillemin and J. Duchesne, "Sur l'origine
asiatique de la cithare grecque," *L'Antiquité classique*, 4(1935):

contradicted by the numerous representations of Hermes as the artist, as in the *Hymn* itself, and also of Apollo as the lyre-maker.[47] It is true that representations of Hermes with the cithara are rare; but Apollo is often associated with the lyre, as he is in the *Hymn*.[48] Every

---

117–24, especially p. 118: "Ces deux instruments, qui se ressemblent par leur forme, diffèrent à l'extrême par leur histoire: alors que la cithare est attestée depuis Sumer jusqu'en Grèce, la lyre fait sa première apparition sur un vase grec de style géométrique." The Greeks credited Terpander (7th century B.C.) with the invention of the seven strings. This chronology is corroborated by the archaeological evidence; cf. Deubner, "Die viersaitige Leier," *Mitteilungen des deutschen archäologischen Instituts, Athenische Abteilung*, 54(1929):197: "Aus der geometrischen Epoche eine Anzahl viersaitige, drei dreisaitige, und eine fünfsaitige Leier nachzuweisen sind, dagegen, soviel ich sehe, keine einzige siebensaitige." Hence Allen and Halliday's dismissal of the lyre as of no significance for the dating of the *Hymn* (*op. cit.*, 275) must be considered as superannuated. The lyre was a house instrument, used at private parties and in the schoolroom, whereas the cithara was a concert instrument, used on sacred occasions and at musical festivals (the distinction is that of Abert, *op. cit.*, 248I). The characteristic function of the lyre is illustrated by the allusion in the *Hymn*, 55–56, to its use at symposia and by the vase-paintings of the "Anacreon" type, which depict an old man, slightly under the influence of liquor, singing and accompanying himself on the lyre; cf. the vases British Museum B192, E266–267, E453–456 (*Corpus Vasorum Antiquorum*, Great Britain 3, British Museum 4, plates 8, 9, 23, 24, 44).

[47] Hermes taught Amphion to play the lyre, according to Eumelus (Pausanias, IX.5.8). For Hermes honored by schoolteachers, along with Apollo, the Muses, and Mnemosyne, see Arrian, *De Venatione*, 34. For Hermes honored by the Dionysiac artists, see Farnell, *Cults*, V, 311, ref. 104f. For the cult of Hermes and the Muses, see W. Dittenberger, *Sylloge Inscriptionum Graecarum* (1st ed., Leipzig, 1883), 349. On the black-figured Attic vase, British Museum B167 (*Corpus Vasorum Antiquorum*, Great Britain 4, British Museum 3, plate 34), Hermes usurps a role generally given to Apollo—the playing of the lyre for Heracles. For Apollo as lyre-maker, see above, note 41.

[48] On the bronze discus in the British Museum (no. 856 in H. B. Walters, *Catalogue of Bronzes, Greek, Roman, and Etruscan, in the British Museum*, London, 1899), the instrument which Hermes has just finished making appears to be a cithara, to judge from the reproduction in Farnell, *Cults*, Vol. V, p. 42, plate VII. A fine example of Apollo and the tortoise-shell lyre is

aspect of music associated with Hermes is also associated with Apollo; and in mythology there is a persistent tendency to advance rival claims on behalf of each of them.[49] In the musical sphere the two cults were not complementary, but in competition. That is why there are representations of Hermes and Apollo literally fighting for possession of the lyre—a myth that carries the rivalry to a more extreme point than does the *Hymn*.[50]

Nor have modern scholars taken seriously the idea in the *Hymn* that Hermes is an intruder into spheres previously reserved for Apollo. Nineteenth-century scholarship tended to explain the variety of attributes ascribed to each of the Greek gods by establishing purely logical connections between them. Hermes' patronage over music was "derived" from his pastoral functions, or from his connection with funeral ceremonies, or from the music-making faculty of the wind, with which Hermes was identified by the school that regarded all the Greek Gods as symbols of natural forces. This method, which reduces Greek religion to a series of syllogisms, leaves no room for the influence of environmental conditions on religion, or for the emergence of genuine novelties in response to changes in the environment. The truth is that while Apollo is represented

---

Ashmolean Museum 524 (*Corpus Vasorum Antiquorum*, Oxford 1, plate 28; Farnell, *Cults*, Vol. IV, p. 328, plate XX). See also Ashmolean Museum 535 (*Corpus Vasorum Antiquorum*, Oxford 1, plate 35); Berlin 2388 (Roscher, *Lexikon der Mythologie*, II, 3245–3246, fig. 2); and Reinach, *Répertoire des vases peints*, II, 30, 44, 76.

[49] Compare also the myth that Apollo first taught Orpheus the lyre (Pindar, *Pythian*, IV.176–177) with the myth that Hermes first taught Amphion the lyre (Eumelus, quoted by Pausanias, IX.5.8).

[50] Lysippus did a bronze group of Apollo and Hermes fighting for the lyre: see Pausanias, IX.30.1, and *Bulletin de correspondance hellénique*, 15 (1891): 399–400. The scene also appears on vases—e.g., Bibliothèque Nationale 820 (Reinach, *Répertoire des vases peints*, II, 259).

as a musician by Homer, Hesiod, and the early lyricists, and also in the earliest archaic art, Hermes' earliest association with music in literature is in Eumelus of Corinth (seventh century B.C.); in art he is not represented as musician until the sixth century, and is not frequently so represented until the fifth century. These facts bear out the idea that Hermes invaded a sphere previously monopolized by Apollo.[51]

At about the same time that Hermes began to be recognized as a musical god, the manner in which he was portrayed in art began to change. In early archaic art Hermes is a bearded, muscular, and rather comical figure—a stylized picture of a man who must work for a living.[52] In the sixth century Hermes begins to lose his beard, and becomes, as Apollo had been before him, the image of the perfect young gentleman, the ideal ephebe, the flower of physical and mental culture, refined by the leisure arts of music and gymnastic—the concept immortalized in the Hermes of Praxiteles.[53] This transformation is already presupposed in the Hymn: Hermes and Apollo, portrayed as rival patrons of young men's musical exercises, are described as "the beautiful sons of Zeus," that is to say, as the two divine symbols of ephebic beauty.[54]

Hermes the god of education and culture is the reli-

---

[51] Eumelus, quoted by Pausanias, IX.5.8; the next literary reference to Hermes as musician is in the Hymn itself. On the date of Eumelus, see Schmid-Stählin, op. cit., Part I, Vol. I, p. 292. On the rarity of representations of Hermes playing the lyre on black-figured vases, see Eitrem, in Pauly-Wissowa, s.v. "Hermes," VIII.765. One instance is British Museum B167 (see note 47 above).

[52] In the Homeric Hymn to Apollo (line 200) Hermes and Ares dance to Apollo's playing of the cithara; in view of Ares' unlovely character and the comical appearance of the archaic, bearded Hermes, this seems to be a satirical thrust at a pair of "uncultured" (ἀπειρόκαλοι) gods.

[53] Cf. Farnell, Cults, V, 44–48; Eitrem, in Pauly-Wissowa, VIII.764, 766–768; Kern, Religion der Griechen, II, 17.

[54] Hymn, 55–56, 323, 397, 504.

gious symbol of the aspirations and achievements of the Greek lower classes. In Aristophanes' *Plutus*, when Chremyles is unexpectedly visited by Wealth, Hermes naturally wants to join the lucky household; after offering himself in various capacities, he is finally accepted as "patron of contests," because "it is most appropriate for Wealth to hold musical and gymnastic contests." Apollo, on the other hand, both as god of music and as the ephebic ideal, was the favorite of the aristocracy, the self-styled "fair and good." When the *nouveaux riches* of the archaic age broke the aristocracy's monopoly of the arts of cultured leisure, they installed their own god as patron of these arts, on a par with Apollo; it was a symbol of their claim to equality: Aristotle regards "culture" (*paideia*) as one of the hallmarks of "the better sort" of citizen, and defines aristocracy as a government in which offices are distributed according to "culture." The resultant transformation of Hermes is reminiscent of the passage in Plato where he so charitably compares "those who associate with culture though unworthy of her" to a little bald tinker who has made a fortune and takes a bath and puts on a new suit, preparatory to marrying his master's daughter.[55]

The representation of Hermes as obtaining equality with Apollo—a representation that was especially provocative because Hermes symbolized the aspirations of the non-aristocratic classes—and the idealization of the acquisitive philosophy which Solon, Theognis, and so many others denounced, were ideas hardly likely to assure the *Hymn* universal acceptance and approval. "The *Hymn* made little or no impression on later literature," one editor says. Its representation of Hermes as the inventor of the lyre was rejected by the partisans of Apollo, including Pindar, Plato, and Callimachus. The

[55] Aristophanes, *Plutus*, 1162–1163; Aristotle, *Rhetoric*, 1365b. 34; Plato, *Republic*, 495E–496A.

idea that Hermes could outwit Apollo was rejected by
Pindar, who firmly states, "No god, no mortal, tricks
Apollo in word or in intention." The very concept of
Hermes the Thief was condemned by Plato—"Theft of
property is conduct unworthy of a free man, and robbery is a shameless act: none of the sons of Zeus ever,
by force or fraud, practised either of these things with
impunity." A more delicate, but none the less palpable,
thrust was made by Sophocles in the *Ichneutai,* a comedy dealing with Hermes' theft of Apollo's cattle:
when the satyr-bloodhounds have followed the scent
right to the door of Maia's cave, the Nymph Cyllene
tries to persuade them that Hermes could not have
been guilty of the theft. "Just consider his lineage," she
says; he is the son of Zeus. Whenever Hermes is represented as the symbol of the acquisitive way of life, he
is inevitably a controversial figure. This is the root of
the derogatory satire which inspires Aristophanes' por-
traits of Hermes; for example, when he puts into Hermes' mouth the cynical epigram that a man's country is
wherever he can do business, he attributes to him a
sentiment profoundly repugnant to the conventional
morality of the audience—witness the fervor with
which the orator Lysias repudiates the same idea in a
speech to an Athenian jury.[56]

In view of the controversial character of the *Hymn,*

---

[56] Allen and Halliday, *op. cit.,* 277; Pindar, *Pythian,* III.29–
30; Plato, *Laws,* 941B; Sophocles, *Ichneutai,* 355; Aristophanes,
Plutus, 1151; Lysias, *Contra Philonem,* 6; Eitrem, "De Mercurio
Aristophaneo," *Philologus,* 68(1909):344–367. The controversial
nature of the god explains the paradox stated, but not solved, by
Nilsson (*Griechische Feste,* 388): "Mit dem Kulte des Hermes
steht es eigentümlich. Er ist ein grosser Gott und ein allgemein
verehrter Gott, in Bild und Lied tausendmal dargestellt, dennoch
hat er wenig Tempel und wenig Feste." That is to say, his popularity was disproportionately greater than his official recognition.
Two possibilities suggest themselves: (1) official circles tended
not to share the popular enthusiasm for Hermes, or (2) official
religious institutions, notoriously conservative, failed to keep
place with Hermes' rise in status and popularity.

it is not surprising to find that the last 78 lines of the
text as it has come down to us are a later addition,
composed by someone who felt that the *Hymn* would
be improved by an ending which placed Apollo in a
more exalted light. The dual authorship is revealed by
a clear break in dramatic continuity, inconsistencies
and duplications in the narrative, and marked stylistic
differences.[57]

The purpose of the Apolline reviser was to present a
different settlement of the relations between Apollo
and Hermes, a "friendship" not predicated, as the exchange scene is, on Hermes' acquisition of equality
with Apollo, but on the application to Hermes of the
Delphic maxim "Know thyself"—don't claim equality
with your betters.[58] Apollo *first* extracts from Hermes
an oath abjuring all designs against Apollo's property,
and then makes certain concessions to him. These are
concessions which give Hermes an inferior status, and
even make him a subordinate of Apollo. Apollo gives
Hermes the magic wand, which in the first part of the
Hymn is assumed to be an aboriginal property of Hermes, and declares that with it Hermes will fulfill all the
ordinances which he, Apollo, pronounces in his capacity as the mouthpiece of Zeus. Then follows a tedious
diatribe in which Apollo explains why Hermes cannot
share his function as the oracle of Zeus (which of
course Hermes nowhere in the *Hymn* asks for), and at
the same time expatiates on the difficulties and respon-
sibilities of his own oracular profession. With obvious
condescension Apollo offers Hermes a kind of divina-

[57] Cf. Radermacher, *op. cit.*, 161–177, 218–219; Humbert,
op. cit., 110–111. The unitarian interpretation is maintained by
Allen and Halliday; on their arguments, see Appendix B.

[58] Plato would call it a friendship based on geometric as opposed to arithmetic equality. The Apollo of the Apolline reviser
says to Hermes what Socrates in the *Gorgias* (508A) says to
Callicles—"You have forgotten that geometric equality is a potent principle both among the gods and among men, and instead
you advocate acquisitiveness."

tion of which, he says, Zeus takes no account—that is
to say, it does not reveal the will of Zeus and hence is
wholly unreliable. Finally, Apollo lists a bewildering
array of animals, wild and domestic, which he places
under Hermes' protection, thus thrusting Hermes
down to the status of a purely rustic cult. With this
settlement Hermes is represented as being content.
This is not the same Hermes who, in the first part of
the *Hymn*, announced his right to equality with Apollo
and his determination to get it by fair means or foul.
His restless pursuit of power after power has been
stilled by the characteristically Delphic virtue of self-
control (*sophrosyne*). The Apolline reviser prefers to
convert Hermes to the Delphic ethic rather than make
Apollo concede equality to Hermes; as Aristotle says,
"It is better to equalize desires than property." His hostility to Hermes remains, however, undiminished: he
concludes by denying Hermes' right to the epithet
"giver of good"—Hermes "does little good, but spends
his whole time cheating the human race." Here we
have that abhorrence of theft and fraud which is part
of the Delphic ethic, but which is conspicuously lacking in the first part of the *Hymn*.[59]

Further light is thrown on the conflict between the
two cults by the nature of the divination transferred
from Apollo to Hermes. It is the art of divination by
mantic dice, an art which the Delphic Oracle once

[59] Aristotle, *Politics,* 1266b.30. The Apolline reviser strikes
the moral note again in line 532; see Radermacher, *op. cit.,* 165.
The emphasis on the doctrine of the mean in the wisdom of the
Seven Sages, who are closely identified with Delphi, is attributed by Barkowski (in Pauly-Wissowa, *s.v.* "Sieben Weisen,"
Part II, Vol. II, p. 2256) to the fact that "Leichtfertigkeit,
Überschwang und Habgier damals schon einen Hauptfehler des
Griechen, insbesondere des Bewohners der grossen Handelstädte
bildeten." Compare the maxims "the love of gain is insatiable,"
"do not get rich the bad way," "loss is preferable to dishonest
gain" (Barkowski, *ibid.,* 2256, 2258). On the Delphic connections of the Seven Sages, see Barkowski, *ibid.,* 2251–2252;
Schmid-Stälin, *op. cit.,* Part I, Vol. I, pp. 373–374.

sanctioned and subsequently rejected, expressing disapproval of it in the words, "There are many who rat-
tle the dice, but there are few who are prophets." The
objection to it was that the use of the mantic dice re-
quired no particular skill; anyone could practice it. It
did not recognize the superiority of the expert in *res
sacrae*, and hence was open to all the objections which
Socrates raised against those who refused to commit
the government of *res profanae* to the few who "have
real knowledge." [60] It is easy to see why the Delphic
Oracle would withdraw its sanction of such a method
of divination when it began to advance the claim that
Delphi was "the navel of the earth," that Apollo was
the "prophet of Zeus," and that the representatives of
the Delphic Oracle in the various Greek cities were the
supreme experts in *res sacrae*.[61] Hermes, on the other
hand, had no such oligarchic principles. He was the
patron of lottery—of which the mantic dice are one
species—and lottery was one of the characteristic institutions of Greek democracy; the extensive use of lottery in the selection of Athenian public officials was the
supreme expression of the democratic principle of the
absolute equality of all citizens.[62]

[60] Zenobius, V. 75; cf. Allen and Halliday, *op. cit.*, 346–347;
Wilamowitz, *Glaube der Hellenen*, I, 379–381; Weniger, in
Roscher, *Lexikon der Mythologie*, *s.v.* "Thriai," V.869; Ehren-
berg, in Pauly-Wissowa, *s.v.* "Losung," XIII.1452–1453; W. R.
Halliday, *Greek Divination* (London, 1913), 210; Parke, *His-
tory of the Delphic Oracle*, 13.

[61] Pindar, *Pythian*, XI.9; Aeschylus, *Eumenides*, 19; Nilsson,
History of Greek Religion, 191–192.

[62] On Hermes as the patron of lottery, compare Aristophanes,
Peace, 365, with the scholia; see also Photius and Hesychius,
s.v. Ἑρμοῦ κλῆρος; Suidas, *s.v.* κλῆρος Ἑρμοῦ. On lottery as a democratic institution, see Aristotle, *Politics*, 1294b.8, and *Rhetoric*,
1365b.32.

CHAPTER

6

ATHENS

The *Homeric Hymn to Hermes* adapts mythological traditions to specific environmental conditions; and the more closely we can define these conditions, the better will be our understanding of the purpose of the *Hymn*. In the preceding chapter it was shown that the unknown author and his audience belonged to the new urban and commercial civilization that was maturing in the archaic age; they must have experienced the rise of the lower classes, their struggle for equality with the aristocracy, and the consequent expansion of the cult of Hermes. These conclusions, which reverse the prevailing opinion that the *Hymn* is the product of a primitive and rustic environment, warrant a fresh attempt to pin its composition down to a particular time and place.

One cannot expect to find in the *Hymn* direct allusions to the historical circumstances under which it was written, but it is not unreasonable to look for allusions

to the religious circumstances. Such an allusion is contained in the detailed account of how Hermes sacri-
ficed two of the stolen cattle. The episode contributes
nothing to the development of the plot; it is the only
passage revealing any interest in the ritual aspect of
religion. The author is plainly attributing to Hermes
the enactment of a ritual which had some special significance for him and his audience.[1]

Hermes' sacrifice takes place beside the ford across
the river Alpheus in Elis, that is to say, on the site of
the great religious center of Olympia; furthermore, he
divides the sacrificial meat into twelve portions. These
details in the narrative make clear that the *Hymn* is
alluding to the famous cult of the Twelve Gods at
Olympia.[2]

Although the *Hymn* unquestionably alludes to the
cult of the Twelve Gods at Olympia, it does not describe it accurately; enough is known about that ritual
to establish the fact that the description in the *Hymn*
is, indeed, quite incompatible with it.[3] In the first place,
the *Hymn* represents Hermes as the founder of the ritual it describes, whereas the undisputed mythical
founder of the cult of the Twelve Gods at Olympia was
Heracles. There is absolutely no evidence of any tradition, either before the *Hymn* or after, attributing to
Hermes any position other than that of being one of
the Twelve Gods.[4] In the second place, Hermes con-

[1] *Hymn,* 106–137.
[2] Weinreich in Roscher's *Lexikon der Mythologie, s.v.* "Zwölf-
götter," VI, 828. Cf. Pindar, *Olympian,* X.49.
[3] This conclusion was first reached by Radermacher (*Der
Homerische Hermeshymnus,* 99) and endorsed by Allen and
Halliday (*The Homeric Hymns,* 305). Neither of them explore
its implications.
[4] Weinreich (in Roscher, *Lexikon der Mythologie, s.v.* "Zwölf-
götter," VI, 764–848), to whose study I am deeply indebted, does
not face squarely the paradoxes of the *Hymn's* relation to the
cult at Olympia. He recognizes that at Olympia the founder was
Heracles, and Hermes merely one of the Twelve (pp. 782–783);
but in trying to reconcile the *Hymn* with the traditions of Olym-

sumes no part of the sacrifice, despite his hunger. Why
—if the *Hymn* is describing the cult at Olympia, where
Hermes was merely one of the twelve recipients—
should he, after carefully making twelve portions, ab-
stain from partaking of the portion belonging to him as
one of the twelve?[5] In the third place, in the *Hymn*
Hermes conducts the sacrifice without the use of an
altar, using a firepit instead; the cult of the Twelve
Gods at Olympia involved altars, very distinctive ones
—six double altars for the Twelve Gods. One of these
double altars was dedicated to Apollo and Hermes together; how could the author of the *Hymn*, which describes the relations of Hermes and Apollo, have failed
to allude to this double altar, if he was thinking of the
Twelve Gods at Olympia?[6] Finally, in the *Hymn* the
fire for the sacrifice is kindled with firesticks; at Olympia, on the other hand, the sacrificial fire was kindled
by ashes taken from the sacred hearth of Hestia.[7]

Obviously the author of the *Hymn* is thinking of the
cult of the Twelve Gods at some place other than
Olympia—doubtless his or his audience's home town.
He has transferred the scene to Olympia, the most fa-

---

pia he denies that Hermes is represented in the *Hymn* as the
founder of the cult (p. 828). Yet when he considers the *Hymn*
by itself he is forced to admit the obvious: "im homerischen
Hermeshymnos, wo offenbar Hermes als Begründer von 12
Götter-Opfern gelten soll" (p. 782).

[5] Radermacher (*op. cit.*, 99) suggests that the *Hymn* was
composed in a place where Hermes had not yet obtained recognition as one of the Twelve Gods. This suggestion presupposes
that the Twelve were originally nameless, a theory refuted by
Weinreich (*op. cit.*, 774–775, 838–840). Cf. Allen and Halliday,
op. cit., 305–306.

[6] See Radermacher, *op. cit.*, 95, 98. On the double altars at
Olympia, see Weinreich, *op. cit.*, 789. Weinreich (pp. 828–829)
argues that the *Hymn* does allude to the double altars; but if it
did, it would certainly use, instead of the phrase "twelve portions," at least the allusive formula of Pindar (*Olympian*, V.5),
"six double altars."

[7] Cf. Farnell, *Cults*, V, 348; L. Weniger, "Die monatliche
Opferung von Olympia," *Klio*, 14 (1915): 398–399.

mous center of the cult of the Twelve Gods, because that location fits in with the topography of the main episode, the theft of the cattle.

The cult of the Twelve Gods was an invention of the archaic age. The selection of twelve gods—a figure based merely on the mystical value of the number—for official canonization and joint worship represented an effort to unify the multifarious devotions of the formerly autonomous communities now integrated into the Greek city-states. The cult of the Twelve Gods at Olympia, to which the *Hymn* alludes, was instituted about 580 B.C., when the city-state of Elis absorbed the territory of Pisa, in which lay the shrine of Olympia. The cult took on a new lease of life in the Hellenistic age, when Hellenistic monarchs and Roman emperors exploited it as a symbol of their overlordship, often adding their own names as the thirteenth god. Most of the known instances of the cult are Hellenistic foundations and therefore have no bearing on the *Hymn*, which reflects the social conditions of the archaic age. In fact, in only one place other than Olympia is the cult known to have existed in the sixth century B.C., and that is Athens. Thucydides says that the altar of the Twelve Gods in the Athenian agora was set up by Peisistratus the younger, grandson of the tyrant Peisistratus, in the year of his archonship, the precise date of which is uncertain, but which in any event was no later than 511 B.C.[8]

---

[8] Thucydides, VI.54. On the geography of the cult, see Weinreich, *op. cit.*, 772–800, and on the nature of the cult, *ibid.*, 767–768, 771–772.

The geography of the cult must be borne in mind when considering other possibilities for the place of composition of the *Hymn*. The cult is not found in Boeotia, where the *Hymn* has sometimes been placed (Allen and Halliday, *op. cit.*, 274). The suggestion that the *Hymn* comes from Ionia (Schmid-Stählin, *Geschichte der griechischen Literatur*, Part I, Vol. I, pp. 236–239) would be supported by Weinreich's theory (*op. cit.*, 829–830) that the cult existed in Ionia before it was introduced on

110   HERMES THE THIEF

The place where the *Hymn* was composed must
have had not only the cult of the Twelve Gods but also
the cult of Hermes; furthermore, to account for a di-
gression on the Twelve Gods in a hymn to Hermes,
and also for the representation of Hermes as the

---

the mainland; but Weinreich's arguments do not stand up under
examination. His first argument is that the cult was more widespread in Asia Minor than on the mainland. But according to
his own tabulation (pp. 772–800), the difference in frequency
is not so very great, thirteen to nine. On the mainland the cult
existed at Olympia, Athens, Salamis, Epidaurus, Thelpusa, Megara, Elatea, Thessaly, Demetrias of the Magnesians; we exclude
Macedonia from the reckoning, include all the islands except
Crete in the total for Asia Minor, and exclude Rhodes and Lycia
as false instances. The greater frequency of the cult in Asia
Minor is explained by the fact that in this area religious institutions were especially subject to *remaniements* in the Hellenistic
age, when the cult was popular as the symbol of Hellenistic
kingship and Roman *imperium*. Furthermore, the mainland instances are older than those of Asia Minor by at least a century.
In only one place in Asia Minor is the cult known to have existed as early as the fifth century B.C., Xanthus in Lycia, and
there it was a direct importation from Athens. At Magnesia on
the Maeander the cult may be as old as the fifth century, but if
so, it was imported from Athens by Themistocles. At Cos, Delos,
and Imbros the cult is attested for the fourth century; at Cos and
Delos it is certainly no older than that. At Eleia in Aeolis the
cult is attested for the second century, and is certainly no older
than the Pergamene monarchy. In seven other cities—Byzan-
tium, Dionysopolis, Laodiceia, Metropolis, Achaion Limen, Lek-
ton, Cyzicus—the cult is attested only for the imperial period.
Cf. Weinreich, *op. cit.*, 787–794, nos. 30–32, 34–35, 41–47, 50.
On the date of the cult at Cos, compare Weinreich, p. 789, no.
34, with Burchner, in Pauly-Wissowa, *s.v.* "Kos," XI.1479. On
the date of the cult at Delos, see R. Vallois, "Topographie
délienne," *Bulletin de correspondance hellénique,* 53(1929):
225–250, 314.
    Weinreich also argues that in view of the inclusion of He-
phaestus and the exclusion of Dionysus in the Twelve, the cult
must have originated in Ionia, where, he asserts, Hephaestus was
indigenous and Dionysus was long regarded as an alien god.
But L. Deubner (*Attische Feste,* 122–123) shows that the
Ionians brought the Dionysiac festival of the Anthesteria with
them in their original migration from Greece to Ionia; the earliest Ionian literature shows complete familiarity with Dionysus
(Heraclitus, Frgs. 14, 15, in Diehl's 3d ed.; Archilochus, Frg. 77,
Alcaeus, Frgs. 10, 96, Anacreon, Frg. 2, all in Diehl); Wilamo-

founder of the cult of the Twelve Gods, there must
have been some special connection between the two
cults. The place that satisfies these conditions is Athens. There both cults existed, and were, moreover, inti-
mately connected. The cult of the Twelve Gods was
centered in the agora: Pindar in his *Dithyramb for the
Athenians* speaks of the Twelve Gods as visiting "the
thronged and incense-fragrant navel of the town in sacred Athens, and the famous agora beautified with
works of art"; the presiding god of the Athenian agora
was Hermes. In the agora stood a number of Hermes
herms; these, with the altar of the Twelve Gods, constituted a religious center that symbolized the unity of
the Athenian state and served as a starting point for
state processions. The two cults also presided over the
network of communications which linked Attica with
the metropolis; the Hermes herms along the country roads of Attica, which served as milestones, bore
inscriptions giving the distance to the altar of the
Twelve Gods.[9]

---

witz (*Glaube der Hellenen*, II, 61) and Nilsson (*Minoan-Mycenaean Religion*, 495) maintain that the cult of Dionysus came to
Greece from Asia Minor. As for Hephaestus, even if we were to
grant the dubious assumption that the role of Hephaestus in
Homer reflects Ionic and not mainland Greek traditions, there are
numerous references to him in Hesiod, and Solon (Frg. 1). Despite the references in Hesiod, Malten, the leading exponent of
the Asiatic origin of Hephaestus, says that there are no traces of
Hephaestus in Boeotia; even he admits, however, that Hephaestus is indigenous in Attica; cf. Malten, in Pauly-Wissowa, *s.v.*
"Hephaistos," VIII.311–313, 325–326. Thus there is no solid
reason for regarding Ionia as the original home of the cult of the
Twelve Gods, and Athens and Olympia remain the two oldest
known centers of the cult.

[9] Pindar, Frg. 63 (ed. Bowra); Xenophon, *Hipparchus*, III.2;
Epigrammata Graeca (ed. Kaibel), 1043. Cf. Judeich, *Topo-
graphie von Athen*, 350; Crome, "Hipparcheioi Hermai," *Mit-
teilungen des deutschen archäologischen Instituts, Athenische
Abteilung*, 60–61 (1935–1936):308–309; A. von Domaszewski,
Die Hermen der Agora zu Athen. Besides Athens and Olympia,
the only places where a cult of both Hermes and the Twelve
Gods is known to have existed before the Roman period are

Athens is the only place where the cults of Hermes
and the Twelve Gods are known to have been interconnected in the manner presupposed by the *Hymn*.
We can go further: Athens is the only place where they
could have been so interconnected in the sixth century
B.C. The only possible basis for a connection between
the two is their common relation to the agora: the
agora is both a commercial and a political center; only
through his relation to the agora can Hermes the god
of commerce make contact with the cult of the Twelve
Gods, the expression of political unity.[10] But the agora,

Delos, Magnesia on the Maeander, Elatea in Phocis, Salamis,
Epidaurus, Imbros, and Calchedon; see Raingeard, *Hermès
psychagogue*, 90, 137, 168, 204, 209–210, 243–250. None of
these places can be seriously considered as the birthplace of the
Hymn. There is no evidence that in any of them either of the
cults existed earlier than the fourth century B.C., nor is there the
slightest trace of any special connection between the two cults.
The only one of these places which has even been suggested as
a possible place for the composition of the *Hymn* is Delos
(Schmid-Stählin, *op. cit.*, Part I, Vol. I, p. 239). The suggestion
was based on the idea that Delos fell within the orbit of the
Ionian culture which is reflected in the *Hymn*, and was a place
where Hermes and Apollo were associated in cult. Apart from
the fact that the cults of Hermes and of the Twelve Gods on
Delos are both of Hellenistic date, and are in no way interconnected, it may be further objected that the forms of cult in
which Hermes and Apollo are associated are purely Hellenistic
forms—the cult of the gymnasium and the cult of the merchant
association, the Hermaistai. In the state cult it is not Apollo
with whom Hermes is associated, but Poseidon (Vallois, *op. cit.*,
233, 314) or Dionysus (P. Roussel, *Délos*, Paris, 1916, p. 233).
For the geography of the cult of Hermes I have relied on
Raingeard, *Hermès psychagogue*, 27–332; Eitrem, in Pauly-
Wissowa, *s.v.* "Hermes," VIII.738–755; and Farnell, *Cults*, V,
76–84.

10 Cf. Weinreich, *op. cit.*, 837: "Als bevorzugter Ort der 12
Götter-Verehrung ergibt sich die Agora"; he instances Athens,
Xanthos in Lycia, Magnesia on the Maeander, Rome, Leontini.
To this list should be added Delos; see Valois, *op. cit.*, 233.
Compare also the tendency to represent the Twelve Gods as an
"Agora of Gods"; see Preller-Robert, I, 111. A. von Premerstein
("Zur Deutung des Parthenonfrieses," *Mitteilungen des deutschen
archäologischen Instituts, Athenische Abteilung*, 38 [1913]):

as we have seen, was not always used as a market-
place, and Hermes' original home was not at the center
but on the edge of things, on the boundary. Nor is it
likely that when the agora became a market-place, official recognition of Hermes as a god of the agora followed immediately and automatically; that position
was already occupied by the gods who had presided
over the agora when it was still exclusively a place of
political assembly, among whom was Apollo.[11] On the
contrary, we must assume that there was a struggle to
win for Hermes official recognition as a god of the
agora; Hermes' claims were advanced by the commercial interests in order to establish a religious sanction
for their ascendancy in the agora and a religious symbol of their political equality; Hermes' intrusion into
the agora paralleled his intrusion into the world of culture. In point of fact, official recognition of Hermes as
a god of the agora seems to have been pioneered by
Athens toward the end of the sixth century B.C.

The characteristic form in which Hermes was represented as god of the agora was the herm, which was an
Athenian invention. The first herms were those that the
tyrant Hipparchus set up about 520–514 B.C. to serve as
milestones along the country roads of Attica. In doing
this Hipparchus integrated the cult of Hermes into the
urban and political life of the city-state. The very form
of the herm reveals, in its affinity with the humble
scarecrow, the recent transference of the cult from the
rural boundaries to the roads leading to the metropolis.
At the same time Hipparchus' herms were symbols of
the unity of the Athenian state: they were inscribed
not only with the distance to the Athenian agora, but

209–222) suggests that the gods on the East Frieze of the Parthenon were represented as an "Agora of Gods."

[11] *Agoraios* is an epithet applied to Zeus (Herodotus, V.46),
Artemis (Pausanias, V.15.4), Athena (Pausanias, III.11.9), and
Apollo (Simonides, Frg. 146, Diehl).

also with gnomic verses embodying Hipparchus' social
ethics; hence they have been rightly described as the
oldest surviving official documents of the Athenian
state. Athens' pioneer role in granting official recognition to Hermes as an urban and political cult was demonstrated again about twenty years after the establishment of the Hipparchan herms, when Athens set up
the first statue to Hermes *Agoraios*. The earliest known
herm from outside Attica comes from the island of
Siphnos, and is dated to about 490 B.C. The earliest
known statue of Hermes *Agoraios* outside of Athens
was a private dedication by the poet Pindar in Thebes
—a dedication seemingly inspired by the cults of the
Athenian agora, which, as we know from his *Dithyramb for the Athenians,* made a deep impression on
him.[12]

In Athens, in the period 520–511 B.C., an altar was
set up to the Twelve Gods in the agora, and the first
Hermes herms, pointing to the agora, were set up
along the roads in Attica. Both Hermes and the Twelve
Gods were honored by new institutions, which brought
them into contact with each other. This is exactly the
situation presupposed by the excursus on the Twelve
Gods in the *Homeric Hymn to Hermes.*

The altar to the Twelve Gods and the Hermes herms
were set up by the Peisistratids. It was under this dynasty of tyrants that Athens became one of the foremost centers of the new industrial and commercial culture, and that the Athenian industrial and commercial

---

[12] Cf. Crome, "Hipparcheioi Hermai," *op. cit.*, 300–313; Goldman, "The Origin of the Greek Herm," *American Journal of
Archaeology,* 46 (1942): 58–68. The Athenians set up a statue
to Hermes *Agoraios* in the archonship of Kebris (Hesychius,
s.v. Ἀγοραῖος), which is dated to the first decade of the fifth
century (Pauly-Wissowa, XI.107). On Pindar's dedication, see
Pausanias, IX.17.2. The antique cult of Hermes *Agoraios* at
Pharai in Achaia (Pausanias, VII.22.2), despite the epithet,
was not of the same type, Hermes' function in the cult being
oracular. The epithet was probably added at a much later time.

classes achieved political equality with the aristocracy.
Solon's redistribution of "status" at the beginning of
the sixth century had not given them equality, and had
failed to put an end to the civil strife. In 581–580 B.C.,
by a compromise agreement between the contending
parties, the archonship was so distributed as to give the
nobility five archons, the farmers three, and the craftsmen two.[13] This is the last we hear of the craftsmen as
an underprivileged, or even as an independent group
in Athenian politics; after the changes wrought by the
tyranny, which was in effect a dictatorship directed
against the aristocracy and supported by the lower
classes, Cleisthenes at the end of the sixth century was
able to base his constitution on the principle that all
Athenians were equal. Social conditions in Peisistratid
Athens corresponded exactly to those presupposed in
the *Hymn.*

In the *Hymn* the aspirations of the industrial and
commercial classes are projected into the figure of
Hermes; their conflict with the aristocracy is projected
into the conflict between Hermes and Apollo. In Athens their aspirations were championed by the tyrant
house, one of whose members, Hipparchus, closely
identified himself with Hermes and was at odds with
Delphi. Hipparchus installed Hermes as the guardian
of the Attic road system; in doing so, according to the
Platonic dialogue the *Hipparchus,* he was motivated
by hostility to Delphi; it is clear that he chose Hermes to
perform a function for which Apollo was equally qual-
ified—Apollo was also a god of ways, of boundaries,
and of the agora, and at a later period there were
Apollo herms. So closely did Hipparchus identify himself with Hermes that the verses he composed for inscription on the herms began with the formula "This is
a monument of Hipparchus"; the Athenians called
them "Hipparchan herms." In the same spirit the con-

[13] Aristotle, *Ath. Pol.,* XIII.2.

temporary painter Epictetus inscribed the dedication "Hipparchus is fair" on his vase depicting a craftsman carving one of the new herms. In Athens under Hipparchus, as in the *Hymn*, Hermes was the symbol of the anti-aristocratic faction.[14]

Throughout their history the cults of Hermes and of the Twelve Gods at Athens were closely interrelated symbols of the popular party and of its hegemony in the state. Hipparchus' promotion of Hermes was part of a general policy of favoring the cults of the lower classes, as was also Peisistratus' promotion of the cult of Dionysus. After the reforms of Cleisthenes had established a democracy in Athens, and as the mercantile interests became increasingly predominant in the state, Hermes was accorded further recognition. The countryside herms were followed by the herms in the agora and by the statue of Hermes *Agoraios*. The herms in the agora were set up as monuments commemorating the military victories of Athenian mercantile imperialism and were used as official starting points for state parades. At the same time they served as party symbols. When on the eve of the Sicilian expedition the

---

14 Plato, *Hipparchus*, 228D–229B; Harpocration, *s.v.* 'Iπ-παρχεῖοι 'Ερμαί. An intimate of Hipparchus was responsible for setting up at Athens the statue of Hermes "with the three heads"; see Philochorus, Frg. 69 (*Fragmenta Historicorum Graecorum*, ed. Muller). On Apollo's epithets, see Farnell, *Cults*, IV, 371, 375; Pausanias, II.35.2; Simonides, Frg. 146 (Diehl); for Apollo herms, see Eitrem, in Pauly-Wissowa, *s.v.* "Hermai," VIII.706. For the background of Hipparchus' hostility to Delphi, see Parke, *History of the Delphic Oracle*, 165–166. The Epictetus vase is dated to 520–510 B.C. by Kraiker ("Epiktetos," *Jahrbuch des deutschen archäologischen Instituts*, 44 [1929]: 175–176). On the identity of the Hipparchus to whom it is dedicated, see E. Langlotz, *Zur Zeitbestimmung der strengrotfigurigen Vasenmalerei und der gleichzeitige Plastik* (Leipzig, 1920), 54–58; C. M. Robinson and E. J. Fluck, *A Study of Greek Love-Names* (Baltimore, 1937), 117–119; and Crome, "Hipparcheioi Hermai," *op. cit.*, 313. Kraiker (*loc. cit.*) identifies him with another member of the Peisistratid family. On Hipparchus and Hermes, see also Cornelius, *Die Tyrannis in Athen*, 60–67.

herms were found to have been mysteriously muti-
lated, the Athenian democrats immediately suspected
an oligarchical conspiracy. Aristophanes, it will be remembered, identifies Hermes *Agoraios* with the mercantile party.[15]

The cult of the Twelve Gods had a parallel history.
Their altar in the agora was set up by one of the Peisistratids, as a symbol of a political unification achieved
at the expense of the aristocracy. The sculptures on the
Parthenon, the supreme artistic expression of the democratic faith of Periclean Athens, include a representation of the Twelve Gods. They also appear on the temple of Victory, as symbols of Athenian power, just as
the herms in the agora were dedicated on the occasion
of Athenian military successes. They were also symbols
of the hegemony of the democratic party in the state.
In Aristophanes' *Knights* Cleon invokes them to sup-
press sedition directed against "the people." Simultane-
ously with the outrage against the herms on the eve of
the Sicilian expedition, an outrage was committed on
the altar of the Twelve Gods. Just as there is a tradition
that Alcibiades was mixed up in the mutilation of the
herms, there is a tradition that Alcibiades "thought little
of the Twelve Gods." [16] So closely is the history of the
two cults intertwined that it is not too much to say that
in a hymn to Hermes produced in Athens an excursus
on the Twelve Gods would be not only permissible but
also mandatory.

Having determined that the *Hymn* was probably
composed in Athens about 520–511 B.C., perhaps we
can, by studying that period more closely, establish a
more definite date for its composition.

Although it is uncertain in what year the younger

[15] Crome, *op. cit.*, 308–309; von Domaszewski, *op. cit.*; Eitrem, in Pauly-Wissowa, *s.v.* "Hermai," VIII.704; Thucydides,
VI.27; Eitrem, "De Mercurio Aristophaneo," *op. cit.*

[16] Aristophanes, *Knights*, 235–236; Plutarch, *Nicias*, 13; Aelius
Aristides (ed. Dindorf), II.369; Weinreich, *op. cit.*, 775–781.

Peisistratus assumed the archonship—when the altar to
the Twelve Gods was set up in the agora—there are
two sound reasons for dating it to the period 514–511
B.C. In the first place, a study of his family tree establishes 544 as the earliest possible date for the birth of
Peisistratus the younger. And since Athenian rule re-
quired that an archon be at least thirty years old, 514 is
the earliest possible date for his archonship. In the second place, it is likely that Peisistratus secured the
archonship during the period when his father Hippias,
Hipparchus' brother, was the sole occupant of the tyranny, i.e., 514–511 B.C. The herms, on the other hand,
were set up by Hipparchus, and Hipparchus was mur-
dered in 514 B.C. Here is a chronological problem. How
could the herms, with their distance readings, have
been set up earlier than the central point to which they
were related, the altar to the Twelve Gods? [17]

The easiest solution to the problem would be to suppose that Peisistratus' altar was not the first altar to the
Twelve Gods in the Athenian agora, and that the
herms were related to an earlier altar in the same
place. But Thucydides speaks of only a single altar,
that which Peisistratus set up; if there had been an earlier one, Thucydides, with his passion for accurate detail and his archaeological interests, would have mentioned it. The conclusion that Peisistratus' altar was the

[17] Cornelius (*Die Tyrannis in Athen*, 10), arguing that the
two foundations must have been simultaneous, insists that on
this account Peisistratus' archonship must be dated to before
514; Weinreich (*op. cit.*, 773) follows Cornelius. Neither of
them attempt to dispose of the arguments for dating the archonship after 514, on which see K. J. Beloch, *Griechische Geschichte*
(Strassburg, Berlin, 1912–27), Vol. I, Part II, p. 300, and
Kirchner, in Pauly-Wissowa, *s.v.* "Peisistratus (4)," XIX.191.
Dr. Charles F. Edson has called my attention to the fact that
B. C. Merritt considered the restoration of [Πεισί]στρατος in a list
of archons, for the year 522–521 B.C. Merritt, however, leaves
the question open, pointing out that there are other names which
would fit, and that it would make Peisistratus a very young
archon indeed; see *Hesperia*, 8 (1939):62.

first has been confirmed by recent excavations of the site. With his permission I quote from a letter from Dr. Homer A. Thompson, the leading authority on the archaeology of the Athenian agora. After making it clear that the exploration of the site is not complete, he says,

With the available evidence, I have been able to distinguish only two periods in the enclosure-wall of the temenos, one pre-Persian and presumably Hipparchan, the other post-Persian. It is quite possible, however, so far as the archaeological evidence goes, that before Hipparchus an altar had stood there with only a wooden fence around it or with none at all. But the dig has given no suggestion of such, nor, to my mind, do the literary references. On general grounds I fail to see the probability of there having been any altar or sanctuary of consequence at this spot before the late sixth century. I'm more and more inclined to associate the altar with an extensive program for the regularization of the region of the Agora at that time. The great stone drain forms the backbone of this scheme; the marble boundary stones, of which the one still stands to the east of the Tholos, are also parts of it. The altar was placed in the fork of an important thoroughfare, the line of which was probably fixed by the laying of the Great Drain.

In view of the evidence we can only conclude that the project of setting up herms between the metropolis and the various villages of Attica came first, and that later, carrying the same centripetal tendency further, came the establishment of the altar. Before they looked to the altar of the Twelve Gods the herms looked to the agora. The excavations have unearthed a massive marble post inscribed, "I am the boundary marker of the agora"; it has been dated to the last decade of the sixth century. This boundary marker shows that the sacred area of the agora was well enough defined to serve as the center from which the distance to the villages was measured. Later, though not more than ten years later than the herms, the "navel" of the town was more exactly defined by the establishment of the altar. This distinction is confirmed by a difference in the distance-indicating formulae on herms of different dates. A fourth-century herm inscription gives the distance to the altar of the Twelve Gods; but the inscription on an original Hipparchan herm says simply, "The glorious Hermes midway between Kephale and the town." [18]

If the establishment of the altar about 514–511 B.C. actually marks the introduction of the cult of the Twelve Gods into Athens, the *Hymn,* in view of its allusion to the cult, must be dated to a time after the establishment of the altar. But, as we saw, the sacrifice to the Twelve Gods in the *Hymn* is conducted without the use of an altar; the *Hymn* must therefore have been composed before the altar was set up, and the cult of the Twelve Gods must have existed in an altarless form before the altar was set up. This inference, which rests on the assumption that the *Hymn* was composed at Athens, is confirmed by a fifth-century inscription which credits Solon with the institution of the cult of the Twelve Gods at Athens. The Athenians of the fifth century, who, as Thucydides shows, knew that Peisistratus the younger had set up the altar, nevertheless believed that Solon founded the the cult; we have no grounds for overriding their opinion. From the time of Solon, therefore, to the archonship of the younger Peisistratus the cult of the Twelve Gods existed in Athens in an altarless form—which is precisely the form of the sacrifice described in the *Hymn.*[19]

---

[18] Thompson, *The Tholos of Athens and Its Predecessors,* 107, 110; *Epigrammata Graeca* (ed. Kaibel), 1043; J. Kirchner and S. Dow, "Inschriften vom attischen Lande," *Mitteilungen des deutschen archäologischen Instituts, Athenische Abteilung,* 62(1937):1–3. It is worth mentioning that line 395 of the *Hymn* has the same hexameter ending as the inscription on the Hipparchan herm: ἀγλαὸς Ἑρμῆς.

[19] The inscription is *Corpus Inscriptionum Graecarum* 452: Σαλαμίνιοι τειχῶς δώδεκα θεοῖς Σόλωνος ("The Salaminians [dedicated] the wall to the Twelve Gods of Solon"). The inscription

The home of the cult of the Twelve Gods in Athens
was the agora; where in the agora was it located before
the altar was set up? It cannot have been housed in a
temple, for if there had been a temple Peisistratus
would have set up his altar there, and not in a separate

---

is now lost, and it is not included in the *Inscriptiones Graecae*.
Weinreich (*op. cit.*, 781) reports that Kirchner is excluding it
from the second edition of the *I.G.*, "weil er die Abschrift für
unzulänglich halt." The word τειχῶς is obviously corrupt, and
was emended by Boeckh to τεῖχος. I see no reason for rejecting
the whole; Dr. Charles F. Edson tells me that Chandler, the
original copyist, is considered conscientious, though not infalli-
ble.

The "Salaminians" who made the dedication were the Athenian citizens who lived in Salamis; the indigenous population,
which lived in a state of serfdom, would have had no reason to
make honorific reference to Solon, the hero of the Athenian conquest of the island; see Busolt-Swoboda, *Griechische Staatskunde*, II, 871. The phrase "the Twelve Gods of Solon" can
refer only to the cult which was the symbol of the Athenian
state. There could be only one cult of the Twelve Gods for all
Athenians, wherever they resided, just as all Athenians, wherever they resided, maintained their membership in the Attic
demes, phratries, and tribes; *ibid.*, 1276. That is why a prayer
to the Twelve Gods was one of the religious formalities prescribed for the dispatching of a new colony; see *Inscriptiones
Graecae* (2d ed.), II, 114. In view of this inscription and another
one found in Salamis which mentions the Twelve Gods (*ibid.*, I,
829), it is probable, though not certain, that there was in
Salamis some sort of shrine to the Twelve Gods; on the other
hand, it is possible that the stone had been removed from Athens
to Salamis, as is suggested by the editor of *I.G.* (I, 829) and
by Weinreich (*op. cit.*, 781). In any case the Twelve Gods honored are those of the Athenian state. Therefore the inscription
attests a belief that Solon founded the Athenian cult.

Weinreich (*op. cit.*, 773) dismisses the belief that Solon had
founded the cult as a legend reflecting the tendency to ascribe
the foundation of Salaminian cults to Solon, the "liberator" of
the island. It must be remembered that Weinreich is prejudiced
by his axiom of the Ionian origin of the cult, which impels him
to date its introduction at Athens to a later period. His argument, which at best shows only that the belief that Solon had
founded the cult may be unhistorical, loses its force in the face
of the fact that it is not a Salaminian cult whose foundation is
attributed to Solon, but the Athenian cult. We have no grounds
for rejecting the testimony of the inscription; see Farnell, *Cults*,
I, 84–85; I. M. Linforth, *Solon the Athenian* (Berkeley, 1919),

precinct. If there was no precinct with an altar, and
no temple, the only possible center was some public
building in the agora. The hypothesis that the cult center was in some such place would explain why it was
altarless. It would resemble the cult of Hestia, the sacred Hearth, a cult that was generally housed in public
or private buildings and was usually altarless because
the sacred fire of the hearth substituted for an altar.

In the fifth century there was in the agora a public
building that was one of the leading centers of Athenian political life, and therefore an eminently suitable
place for a cult symbolizing the unity of the state. This
was the Tholos, sometimes called the Prytanikon, the
official residence of the Prytanes, the presiding officers
of the Boule or Council. In fact, there is some evidence
suggesting that there was a cult of the Twelve Gods in
the Tholos. The Tholos was the scene of ritual actions,
sacrifices, and libations performed by the Prytanes. We
are told that it contained certain small silver images
with statues of heroes close by; some archaeologists believe that the images were those of the Twelve Gods of
the state, placed there to complement the statues of the
heroes of the state. In Hellenistic times there was a
tendency to imagine an affinity between the Ruler cult
—so often associated with the cult of the Twelve Gods
—and the circular type of building called a Tholos; it is
likely that the same cycle of ideas was reflected in the

256. Quite apart from the evidence of the inscription, the general nature of the cult of the Twelve Gods, as the symbol of
political unity, makes it probable that Solon rather than Peisistratus the younger introduced it at Athens. If Solon introduced
it, it would have been as a religious sanction for his new constitution or for the conquest of Salamis, just as it was introduced
at Olympia, at about the same time, to sanction the absorption
of Pisa by Elis and the consequent reorganization of the shrine
of Olympia. In the archonship of Peisistratus the younger there
was no such reason for introducing the cult; if, however, it had
been introduced by Solon, further expansion of the cult would
always be appropriate.

cults of the most famous Tholos, the Tholos at Athens. At Magnesia on the Maeander—where, according to some authorities, the cult of the Twelve Gods was introduced by Themistocles and was modeled on the Athenian cult—a wooden Tholos was erected in the agora for the Twelve Gods at the annual festival of Zeus the "Savior of the City." [20]

The Tholos in the Athenian agora was built about 470 B.C. Recent excavations, however, have revealed that the Tholos was preceded by a series of sixth-century buildings occupying the same site and serving the same purpose. According to Homer Thompson's reconstruction, approximating the time of the reforms of Solon—which is also the period when the cult of the Twelve Gods was introduced at Athens—a building was erected in the southwest corner of the agora which served as the headquarters of the Boule, a "primitive Bouleuterion." In the third quarter of the sixth century, during the Peisistratid period, a primitive Prytanikon was constructed around this Bouleuterion. Until replaced by the Tholos, this Prytanikon was the dining hall of the Prytanes, and there is definite archaeological evidence that it was the scene of ritual actions, just as the Tholos was.[21]

The construction of the Bouleuterion in the time of Solon and of the Prytanikon in the time of the Peisistratids represented a deliberate effort on the part of the nascent Athenian democracy to promote the agora at the expense of the Acropolis, where public life had been concentrated under earlier regimes. The new buildings in the agora were the counterpart of the old

[20] Demosthenes, XIX.190; Pausanias, I.5.1; O. Kern, *Inschriften von Magnesia* (Berlin, 1900), 98; Judeich, *Topographie von Athen*, 346; Nilsson, *Griechische Feste*, 23; Thompson, *The Tholos of Athens and Its Predecessors*, 137–141; Fiechter, in Pauly-Wissowa, *s.v.* "Tholos," Part II, Vol. VI, p. 312; Weinreich, *op. cit.*, 838.
[21] Thompson, *The Tholos of Athens*, 39–44.

Prytaneion on the Acropolis, which had been the headquarters of the monarchy and the aristocracy.[22] In the
old Prytaneion there was a perpetual fire sacred to
Athena, the goddess of the city, and to Hestia, the
symbol of patriarchal or familial unity.[23] The new
public center in the agora had to be sanctified by new
religious institutions. What could be more appropriate
than to introduce the cult of the Twelve Gods, the
symbol of political as opposed to patriarchal unity, in
an altarless form reminiscent of the cult of Hestia in
the Prytaneion? There is an exact parallel in the foundation of the cult of the Twelve Gods at Olympia, at
about the time of Solon's reforms. At Olympia, as at
Athens, the cult of Hestia had been the original symbol
of unity. When Elis absorbed Olympia into a wider
political entity, and the sacred area was placed under
the protection of the Twelve Gods, the memory of
Hestia as the parent symbol of unity was preserved by
giving her a preeminent position among the Twelve
Gods: sacrifice was made to her first and last, and
from her sacred hearth ashes were taken to light the
altar of Zeus *Olympios*, the first of the Twelve Gods.[24]

In the third quarter of the sixth century—a period
which extended into Hipparchus' tyranny—the cult of
the Twelve Gods, which since its introduction by Solon
must have been housed in the Bouleuterion, was trans-

[22] See J. Charbonneaux, "Tholos et Prytanée," *Bulletin de
correspondance hellénique*, 49(1925):158–178.

[23] Farnell, *Cults*, V, 347; Suss, in Pauly-Wissowa, *s.v.*
"Hestia," VIII.1283–1292.

[24] Farnell, *Cults*, V, 348; Weniger, "Die monatliche Opferung
von Olympia," *Klio*, 14(1915):398–399. There is other evidence
of close affinity between the cult of Hestia in the Prytaneion and
the cult of the Twelve Gods in the agora at Athens: both cults
were approached when a colony or cleruchy was being sent out;
see Herodotus, I.146; *Inscriptiones Graecae*, 2d ed., II, 114;
Farnell, *Cults*, Vol. V, p. 370, Ref. 30. Both cults furnished a
refuge for suppliants; see Diodorus, XIV.4; Herodotus, VI.108;
Weinreich, *op. cit.*, 773.

ferred to the new Prytanikon.[25] Soon thereafter, about
520–514, the herm cult was established. Both events
reflected the Peisistratid policy of developing the agora
as a political center. This is the historical setting of the
excursus on the Twelve Gods in the *Homeric Hymn to
Hermes*.

This setting explains all the peculiarities of the ritual
described in the *Hymn*—Hermes' abstention from eating his portion, the kindling of the sacrificial fire with
firesticks, and the use of a firepit instead of an altar.
In describing the sacrifice the *Hymn* represents
Hermes in his traditional role of "herald," or ceremonial functionary. There is an exact parallel in the ritual
at Athens, where it was customary for the herald to
represent the state in intercessions to the Twelve Gods.
The affiliation of the altarless sacrifice to the Twelve
Gods with the altarless sacrifice to Hestia explains why
Hermes did not eat. No one partook of a sacrifice to
Hestia; the Greeks had a proverb, "He is sacrificing
to Hestia," the point of which was that in sacrificing to
Hestia no one received a share of the sacrifice.[26]

The relation of the cult of the Twelve Gods to the
cult of Hestia also suggests a reason for the use of the
firesticks. The cult of Hestia is the cult of a central
hearth on which all members of a family depend for

25 Before the construction of the Prytanikon the cult of the
Twelve Gods must have been housed in the primitive Bouleuterion. Thompson (*op. cit.*, 43) points out that the primitive
Bouleuterion was too small to have served as the meeting place
of the Boule. He suggests that it housed "the records, seals, and
other permanent equipment of the Boule"; their permanent
equipment would have included cult objects. In the same way
the sixth-century complex of buildings must have housed the
public measures which were instituted by Solon (Aly, in Pauly-
Wissowa, *s.v.* "Solon," Part II, Vol. III, p. 976), and which
were found in the excavations of the fifth-century Tholos
(Thompson, *op. cit.*, 141–142).

26 *Inscriptiones Graecae*, 2d ed., II, 112, 114; *Paroemiographi
Graeci* (ed. Leutch and Schneidewin), I, 97 (Zenobius).

fire. At Olympia Hestia retained a preeminent position as a symbol of unity because her hearth remained the only source of fire—from it were taken ashes to light the altars of the Twelve Gods. At Athens, on the other hand, Hestia stayed in the Prytaneion on the Acropolis, where, if her fire went out, it was rekindled directly from the sun by means of a burning-glass. In the cult of the Twelve Gods in the Prytanikon in the agora, if the *Hymn* is accepted as evidence, the sacrifice was kindled by firesticks, as was the sacred fire tended by the "Virgins of the Hearth," the Vestal Virgins, in Rome. The use of the firesticks distinguished the cults of the Prytanikon from those of the Prytaneion; by sanctifying a new method of producing fire it emancipated the citizenry from its dependence on the ancestral Hearth on the Acropolis. Having this significance, the firesticks merit the attention given them in the *Hymn*.[27]

Instead of an altar, Hermes uses a firepit to cook the sacrificial meat, "a pit in the ground." In the sixth-century complex of buildings on the site of the fifth-century Tholos the American excavators unearthed a pair of long firepits, which, according to Homer Thompson, had "served the archaic complex through most of its history." There is no doubt that the pits were used for broiling meat, for the bottoms were covered with ash and charcoal and the bones of animals identifiable as cows, sheep or goats, pigs, and deer. The firepits of the sixth-century Prytanikon, primarily intended for the cooking of the meat served at the banquets of the Prytanes, had also a ceremonial function. The common banquets of the Prytanes were themselves ceremonial in character; Demosthenes, for instance, speaks of occasions when "all the Prytanes make a common sacrifice together and dine together and pour libations together." The firepits were conspic-

[27] Plutarch, *Numa,* 9; Athenaeus, 530E; Farnell, *Cults,* V, 351–354, 360. Cf. also Apollonius Rhodius, *Argonautica,* I.1184.

uously placed in a large open space between the Prytanikon and the Bouleuterion—the space where, according to Homer Thompson, the old Boule met. Such
a conspicuous place for a broiling-pit would be appropriate if the broiling was sometimes ceremonial.[28]

The excursus on the Twelve Gods, important as it is,
is not the only clue to the place where the *Hymn* was
composed. As we saw in the preceding chapter, the
tribute the *Hymn* pays to Hermes as a god of music,
culminating in the claim that Hermes is the consort of
Mnemosyne, the mother of the Muses, is unique in
Greek literature. Since, as we saw, recognition of
Hermes as a musical god began only at the end of the
seventh century, and was not widespread until the

---

[28] *Hymn*, 112; Demosthenes, XIX.190; Thompson, *op. cit.*,
16, 25–27, 41, 43; see also Farnell, *Cults*, V, 350–351; Suss, in
Pauly-Wissowa, *s.v.* "Hestia," VIII.1285. Radermacher (*Hermeshymnus*, 93, 222) regards the mention of the firepit as further proof of the "primitive" character of the *Hymn:* "Wohl
aus persönlicher Erfahrung spricht der Dichter von einer Form
des Herdes, die in Europa sicher die älteste ist."
  In addition to the firepits, the excavators of the Prytanikon
unearthed a very curious object called by Homer Thompson
"the round poros monument." It is a tapering object, its lower
diameter being 0.75 m., its upper diameter 0.71 m. Originally
it consisted of one drum, 0.56 m. high, with a sort of peg pro-
truding from it; later a second drum was placed on top. The
lower drum is a well-finished job, with smooth surfaces and
neatly beveled edges. Its purpose, says Thompson (*op. cit.*,
39–40), "is not, perhaps never will be certain." The passage
in the *Hymn* describing Hermes' sacrifice mentions several sacred stones: (1) Hermes stretched the hides "on a hard dry
rock," "where they remain to this day" as relics (lines 124–
126); (2) Hermes placed the meat on a "smooth flat surface,"
which he used as a butcher's block (lines 127–128); (3) the
twelve portions were placed somewhere high up inside the
"high-roofed chamber" as a "monument to his recent theft"
(lines 131–136). Since the twelve portions of "meat and fat" are
relics, the writer of the *Hymn* must have had in mind something in stone which represented twelve portions of meat. See
Allen and Halliday, *op. cit.*, 273, 304, and Radermacher, *op.
cit.*, 95, 100, 190. Perhaps a consideration of this passage in the
Hymn in connection with the "round poros monument" may
serve to extend the scope of speculation about the purpose of
the latter.

fifth, in the sixth century only a limited number of communities would have been willing to accept the claims put forward in the *Hymn*. If we were right in thinking that Hermes' intrusion into the musical sphere paralleled the initiation of the lower classes into the cultured pursuits previously monopolized by the aristocracy, then in the place where the *Hymn* was composed the lower classes must have already achieved a measure of cultural quality.

A recent historian of the Athenian tyrant house singles out as the most important achievement of the Peisistratids the termination of the aristocratic monopoly of cultural pursuits and the establishment of institutions that made literature, music, and athletics available to the lower classes; to the Peisistratids he gives the main credit for the phenomenally high cultural level of the Athenian people as a whole in the fifth century. Specific Peisistratid measures directed toward this objective were the introduction of literary performances in the program of certain public festivals and the construction of public gymnasia where all the people could practice the arts that had previously been reserved for the few.[29]

One of these public gymnasia was the work of Hipparchus. Constructed at so great an expense that it became a byword for extravagance, the public gymnasium in the Academy served the population of the Kerameikos, the potters' district—a center of Athenian industry. What gods did Hipparchus install as the patrons of his new gymnasium? Pausanias says, "In the Academy there is an altar to Prometheus, and there is an altar to the Muses, and another to Hermes, and, inside, one to Athena and another to Heracles." Athena is of course the goddess of the state; Prometheus is a particular favorite of the Athenian potters; and the gods invoked as the patrons of culture are the Muses,

[29] Cornelius, *Die Tyrannis in Athen*, 65–67.

Hermes, and Heracles. Apollo does not appear, as he so often does, as the companion of the Muses or of Heracles. Instead we have Hermes associated with the Muses, the Hermes of the *Hymn*, who sings "first of Mnemosyne, the mother of the Muses, for she drew the son of Maia as her lot." [30]

Another artistic tribute to the cults of Hipparchus' gymnasium comes, naturally enough, from one of the Athenian potters. There is a sixth-century Attic vase which depicts Hermes playing the lyre for Heracles' entertainment, one of the extremely rare representations in the black-figured style of Hermes playing the lyre. It shows that Athens was one of the few places where Hermes was recognized as a musical god in the sixth century. In playing for Heracles' entertainment Hermes usurps a role generally attributed to Apollo in the black-figured style, just as in the cults of Hipparchus' gymnasium he usurps Apollo's position as the companion of Heracles and the Muses.[31]

[30] See Suidas, *s.v.* τὸ Ἱππάρχου τειχίον; Pausanias, I.30.2; Weber, "Kerameikos-Kulte," *Mitteilungen des deutschen archäologischen Instituts, Athenische Abteilung,* 50 (1925):139–156; Solders, *Die ausserstädtische Kulte,* 58, 138. Weber holds that Hipparchus merely remodeled the gymnasium, Cornelius that he founded it. The difference is of slight importance (Weber attributes the foundation to Peisistratus), but Cornelius' view seems preferable, since it is hard to think of a gymnasium without a wall around it. Further evidence of the Peisistratid interest in the cults of the place is the fact that another member of the family, Charmos, set up an altar to Eros at the entrance to the Academy; see Athenaeus, 609D, and Weber, *op. cit.,* 140. It was also in the Kerameikos that one of Hipparchus' intimates set up the statue of Hermes "with the three heads"; see Philochorus, Frg. 69 (*Fragmenta Historicorum Graecorum,* ed. Muller); Hesychius, *s.v.* Ἑρμῆς τρικέφαλος.

[31] British Museum B167 (see above, page 98, note 47). Apart from Athens, there are, so far as I can see, only three other places where there is known to have been an association between Hermes and the Muses in cult: (1) the cult of Hermes, Apollo, and the Muses at Megalopolis (Pausanias, VIII.32.2); (2) Hermes, Apollo, and the Muses in the cult of the Dionysiac artists at Opus (*Inscriptiones Graecae,* IX, 1.278, an inscription of the second century B.C.); and (3) Hermes, Heracles, and the

The case for placing the composition of the *Hymn* in Hipparchan Athens would be incomplete without taking account of an allusion that has suggested an argument for a different location. The mention of the shrine of Poseidon at Onchestos in Boeotia, as the home of the "old man who couldn't hold his tongue"—originally an Arcadian figure—is quite gratuitous and indicates a special interest in the place. This allusion, combined with a few supposed traces of Boeotian dialect, has led some scholars to suggest that the *Hymn* was composed in Boeotia. Traces of Boeotian dialect, however, are not incompatible with the composition of the *Hymn* at Athens; Hipparchus attracted poets from all over Greece to his court. The allusion to Onchestos is also perfectly appropriate in a poem composed with an eye on Hipparchus' achievements and interests. Boeotia was for a long time a staunch ally of the Peisistratids; the Theban aristocracy contributed toward the financing of Peisistratus' return from exile; Hipparchus and Hippias stayed at Eretria in Euboea—just off the coast of Boeotia—during the exile. The shrine of Poseidon at Onchestos and the shrine of Apollo at Ptoion were the two cult centers of the Boeotian confederacy. At Ptoion, in order to consolidate his ties with Boeotia, Hipparchus made a dedication the base of which, inscribed *Hipparchos,* has been discovered by archaeologists. The allusion to Onchestos in a hymn composed for presentation at Athens may represent a similarly friendly gesture toward a political ally; in any case it

---

Muses in the cult of the ephebes in Teos (W. Dittenberger, *Sylloge Inscriptionum Graecarum* [1st ed., Leipzig, 1883], 349, an inscription of the third century B.C.). The cults of Megalopolis and Opus are certainly no older than the fourth century B.C.; the foundation of the cult at Teos, attested only for the third century, cannot be dated. For the instances of Hermes associated with the Muses in cult see Raingeard, *Hermès psychagogue,* index, *s.v.* "Muses."

would strike a responsive chord in Hipparchus' circle.[32]

The Peisistratid friendship with Boeotia came to an end about 519 B.C., in a dispute over the border town of Plataea. If the mention of Onchestos in the *Hymn* was inspired by the same political considerations that prompted Hipparchus' dedication at the shrine of Ptoion, then the allusion makes 519 the latest possible date for the composition of the *Hymn*, just as the allusion to the connection between Hermes and the Twelve Gods makes 520 B.C. the earliest possible date.

The references to Hipparchus' activities—the friendship with Boeotia, the construction of the gymnasium in the Academy, the establishment of the cult of the Twelve Gods in the Prytanikon, the foundation of the herm cult—are so numerous as to raise the question whether the *Hymn* did not have a closer relation to the tyrant than the mere circumstance of its composition in Athens during his reign. For what occasion was it composed? Not for a ritual occasion, it would appear, if one may argue from the fact that, unlike the *Homeric Hymns* to Apollo and Demeter, it fails to describe any rituals of the god it celebrates. More plausible seems the hypothesis that it was intended for performance at a private festivity. The inclusion of a hymn in the program of a banquet was an ancient Greek custom, and at least one other of the *Homeric Hymns* was written for such a private occasion. The theory that the *Hymn* had a similar purpose is supported by the prom-

---

[32] *Hymn*, 88, 186. The theory that the Hymn originated in Boeotia is advanced, with varying degrees of conviction, by Radermacher (*op. cit.*, 233), Allen and Halliday (*op. cit.*, 274–275) and Humbert, *Homère Hymnes*, 112–113. On the relations between the Peisistratids and Boeotia, see Herodotus, I.61; Cornelius, *op. cit.*, 46, 50; Schachermeyr, in Pauly-Wissowa, *s.v.* "Peisistratus," XIX.183; L. Bizard, "Inscriptions du Ptoion; 2: Les Pisistratides au sanctuaire," *Bulletin de correspondance hellénique*, 44(1920):237–241; and J. J. E. Hondius, "Hippias oder Hipparchos," *Hermes*, 57(1922):475–477.

inence given the lyre and the vivid references to its use at symposia, which would then have much more point. These features of the *Hymn*, together with the references to Hipparchus' activities, suggest that it was composed for private performance at the court of the tyrant.[33]

If the *Hymn* was composed for Hipparchus and his court, we should expect the tastes of this intimate audience to have influenced not only its content but also its style. If we analyze the salient stylistic characteristics of the *Hymn* in the light of what is known about the tastes and interests of Hipparchus' circle, we shall have to concede that the *Hymn* has all the earmarks of a piece designed to please the fancy of this slightly eccentric group.

Among these salient stylistic characteristics is the sophisticated humor of the *Hymn*, which one critic has not inaptly compared to "a miracle-play written by Congreve." The subject—the conflict between Hermes and Apollo—has real religious and ethical significance; but to enlist the sympathies of the audience on the side of Hermes the poet appeals chiefly to their sense of humor. With sophisticated detachment he exploits traditional mythological concepts for comic effect: in the narrative of the cattle theft the numerous illogicalities that the eagle eye of scholarship has detected only show how little interested the author was in verisimilitude, which he willingly sacrifices to his humorous embroidery, Hermes' smartness and Apollo's bewilderment.[34]

[33] On the performance of hymns at private festivities, see *Homeric Hymn* XXIV.4; Schmid-Stählin, *op. cit.*, Part I, Vol. I, p. 340; Wünsch, in Pauly-Wissowa, *s.v.* "Hymnus," IX.145, 147. Cf. the command performances at royal banquets, for example Demodocus' lay in the *Odyssey*.

[34] Rose, *Handbook of Greek Mythology*, 147. On the illogicalities, see Robert, "Zum homerischen Hermeshymnos," *Hermes*, 41(1906):389–425, and the criticism of Robert by Kuiper in "De discrepantiis Hymni Homerici in Mercurium," *Mnemosyne*,

Of all the comic effects achieved in the *Hymn* the
most striking are the subtle and successful ventures
into humor of the risqué type. In the invocation it is
said that Zeus used to sleep with Maia for as long as he
could while his wife Hera was sleeping. When Hermes
first plays on the lyre, "trying his skill at improvisation,
just as youthful revellers at banquets match their wits
in alternate sallies,"

> *He sung how Jove and May of the bright sandal*
> *Dallied in love not quite legitimate;*
> *And his own birth, still scoffing at the scandal,*
> *And naming his own name, did celebrate.*

But the most daring example is the personification of
the lyre. Hermes first greets the lyre with the words,
"Welcome, dancer with the lovely figure, companion of
the banquet"; later he tells Apollo to take her to the
banquet and the dance and the revel, promising that
she will be to him "a joy both night and day": he describes her, without further equivocation, as a "shrill-
voiced companion"—literally, a "shrill-voiced hetaera."
The true character of the personified lyre has escaped
the notice of the commentators; in the simple rustic
society in which they believe the *Hymn* was produced
a hetaera would indeed be a monstrosity. In these ventures into erotic humor, as in the description of the
omen which Hermes emitted to make Apollo drop him
—"an unfortunate servant of the belly, an impudent
messenger"—the *Hymn* comes as close to the Aris-

---

n.s., 38(1910):1–50. Kuiper's conclusion on the poet's style is
worth quoting: "Nunc parodia usus, nunc pro antiqua fide reli-
gionis rationem mentis suae substituens, conjungit diversa, sepa-
rat conjuncta" (p. 24). See also Radermacher, *op. cit.*, 212:
"Das Ganze für ihn nur ein Spielmotiv der Diebsgeschichten
war, von dem mehr zum Ergötzen einer nicht gerade kritisch
gestimmten Zuhörerschaft Gebrauch gemacht wird." What the
audience was uncritical about is the verisimilitude of his picture
of cattle-stealing.

tophanic manner as is possible in the "Homeric" style.[35]

A third stylistic feature of the *Hymn* is the frequent parody of Homer and Hesiod. The verbal humor is for the most part based on a calculated incongruity between the subject matter and the epic language used. For example, the formula "craving meat," applied in the *Iliad* to a ravenous lion, is used to describe the newborn baby setting out after Apollo's cattle. The whole scene of Hermes and the tortoise is modeled on Hesiod's parable of the hawk and the nightingale, and culminates with the classic parody of the Hesiodic maxim, "It is better to stay at home, since the outside world is noxious." To appreciate such parodies the original audience of the *Hymn* must have been literary-minded, just as it must have been musically inclined to relish the discussion of the merits of the lyre and the techniques of lyre-construction and lyre-playing.[36]

To describe Hipparchus' character Aristotle uses three terms—"gay," "amorous," and "devoted to literature and music." Who can deny that the audience for which the *Hymn* was composed shared all these attributes? The licentious gaiety of Hipparchus' banquets is preserved for us in the symposiastic scenes on the bases of the court painter Epictetus: there we can see the

---

[35] *Hymn,* 7–8, 55–59, 31, 477–482; cf. Radermacher, *op. cit.,* 59, 66; Allen and Halliday, *op. cit.,* 281, 289–290, 448. In line 31 "companion of the banquet" is, of course, an epic formula for the lyre (see *Odyssey,* 17.271), but in view of the parodistic tone of the context, and the phrase "dancer with the lovely figure," I believe the sophisticated audience would catch a *double entendre.* It is otherwise with the "shrill-voiced companion" of line 478; how can it mean the same thing as "companion of the banquet" in *Odyssey,* 17.271? Yet the silence of the commentators indicates that this is the way they take it.

[36] *Hymn,* 64, 25–40. See Boettcher, *De Hymno in Mercurium Homerico;* also Radermacher, *op. cit.,* the pages indexed under "Ausdrucksweise, bewusst komische" and "Parodie." Robert (*op. cit.,* 391–398) also discusses the element of parody, but his distinction of two styles (and two authors) is groundless (apart from lines 512–580, the work of the Apolline reviser, in which there is no parody and no humor). See Kuiper, *op. cit.,* 19.

"youthful revellers" and the "shrill-voiced hetaera" of
the *Hymn*. Hipparchus' literary interests expressed
themselves not only in occasional verse by the tyrant
himself, but also in his patronage of Anacreon, Simonides, Lasos, Onomacritus, and "other poets"—among
whom I count the author of the *Hymn*.[37]

Hipparchus' literary circle brought the new Ionian
art, the outgrowth of the new commercial culture
which first matured in the coastal cities of Asia Minor,
to Athens. Among the artistic novelties developed by
the Ionians was the lyre. At Athens, at the beginning of
the sixth century, as Solon's verses show, poetry composed for recital at banquets and other private social
occasions was in the elegiac meter, and was accompa-
nied by the flute. The flute elegy, earnest and didactic
in tone, had been the favorite poetic form of the great
aristocracies of the seventh century on the mainland;
before Solon its leading exponents had been Tyrtaeus of
Sparta and Theognis, the apologist of the aristocrats of
Megara. In Ionia, meanwhile, a more personal and
more sophisticated style of poetry for private social occasions was being developed by such artists as
Terpander and Alcaeus, who used various melic meters
and, as accompaniment, the lyre or that very similar
instrument the barbitos. In the second half of the sixth

[37] Aristotle, *Ath. Pol.*, XVIII.1; cf. Cornelius, *op. cit.*, 58, 68,
72–75, 78, 80; Kraiker "Epiktetos," *Jahrbuch des deutschen
archäologischen Instituts*, 44 (1929):141–197; Herodotus, VII.
6. The pseudo-Platonic *Hipparchus* (228 B–C) attributes to
Hipparchus the introduction of Homeric recitals at the Pan-
athenaea. Although this statement can hardly be accepted at
its face value (see Schmid-Stählin, *op. cit.*, Part I, Vol. I, p.
159; Vol. II, p. 24; Cornelius, *op. cit.*, 72–75), it does suggest
that Hipparchus' literary interests included, in addition to lyric
and theogonic poetry, the type called Homeric. At any rate a
study of the choice of subjects in Attic vase-painting of the
sixth century shows that Athens began to be familiar with
Homer about 560 B.C.; see Zschietzschmann, "Attische Bildkunst um 560," *Jahrbuch des deutschen archäologischen Instituts*, 46 (1931):45–60.

century the Ionian style of melic lyric came to Athens. An Attic vase of the sixth century depicts Athena, the symbol of Athens, with a tortoise-shell lyre in her hand, inscribed *lyre* to advertise the novelty. The drinking songs of the aristocrats who conspired against Hippias and Hipparchus are in the melic form. At Athens, therefore, in the age of Hipparchus, the *Hymn's* praise of the lyre as a symposiastic instrument superior to the flute was a timely theme. But here again the *Hymn* was aimed directly at Hipparchus. In the musical circle around the tyrant the issue of lyre versus flute was a lively one, with Hipparchus favoring the lyre: Anacreon, of all these poets the most sympathetic to Hipparchus, was remembered in Athens long after his death as "the opponent of the flutes, the lover of the barbitos." [38]

The artists who visited Hipparchus' court brought, too, new Ionian versions of old myths. In Ionia at the beginning of the sixth century Alcaeus had sung of Hermes' theft of Apollo's cattle, and toward the middle of the century the scene had been depicted on one of the Caeretan Hydriae. At Athens toward the end of the sixth century two vase-paintings reinterpret the scene on the Caeretan Hydria, and about 520 B.C. the *Hymn* reinterprets the theme of Alcaeus' *Hymn to Hermes*.[39]

_____

[38] *Hymn,* 55–56, 452–455; Critias, Frg. 8 (Diehl); J. C. Hoppin, *Handbook of Greek Black-Figured Vases* (Paris, 1924), 60, Archikles no. 3; Schmid-Stählin, *op. cit.,* Part I, Vol. I, pp. 238, 332, 337–338, 347–350, 356, 442; Wilamowitz, *Pindaros,* 96; Abert, in Pauly-Wissowa, *s.v.* "Saiteninstrumente," Part II, Vol. I, p. 1764. Compare also the vases depicting Alcaeus and Sappho with the barbitos, e.g., Reinach, *Répertoire des vases peints,* I, 524–526. The earliest literary mention of the word "lyre" is in Archilochus, Frg. 51 (Diehl); the next mention is in the *Hymn.*

[39] On Alcaeus' hymn and the Caeretan Hydria, see above, page 78, note 11. The two Attic vases are the Brygos vase in the Vatican and a black-figured Athenian amphora depicting Hermes and the oxen of Apollo, which is now in the Metropolitan Museum of Art (No. GR529; see frontispiece and

By 520–519 B.C., the date of the *Hymn*, we find
Hermes under the protection of the tyrant house of
Athens, his cult established as one of the political cults
of the Athenian state, his aptitude for the cultural life
given recognition by Hipparchus in his new gymnasium, his new successes immortalized by one of the
poets who brought the Ionian spirit to Athens.[40]

A. Hoeber, *The Treasures of the Metropolitan Museum of Art*,
New York, 1899, p. 47); Miss Richter tells me that it belongs
to the late sixth century B.C. So far as I know, these three are
the only archaic vases illustrating the myth of Hermes' cattle-
theft. It is noteworthy that the amphora in the Metropolitan
Museum depicts Hermes as a beardless youth, proof that the
concept of Hermes as the ideal ephebe, presupposed in the
Hymn (see above, p. 96) was current in Athens at the end of
the sixth century. For another Attic vase-painting of the late
sixth century which depicts Hermes as an ephebe, see Beazley,
Attic Red-Figure Vase-Painters, 928, and Robinson and Fluck,
A Study of Greek Love-Names, 125-126.

[40] There are other arguments that confirm the date, though
not the place, which we have assigned to the composition of
the *Hymn:* (1) The *Hymn* alludes to the cult of the Twelve
Gods at Olympia, which, acording to the leading authority, was
instituted about 580 B.C.; see L. Weniger, "Olympische Studien," *Archiv für Religionswissenschaft,* 20(1920–21):41–78.
(2) Line 178 of the *Hymn,* where Hermes threatens to plunder Pytho, is probably an allusion to the events of the first
Sacred War, about 590 B.C.; see Schmid-Stählin, *op. cit.,* Part
I, Vol. I, p. 238. (3) The *Hymn* makes a number of allusions
to the *Homeric Hymn to Apollo,* which there are good reasons
for dating to a time later than 590 B.C.; see Radermacher,
op. cit., 110, 229; Dornseiff, "Zum homerischen Hermeshymnos," *Rheinisches Museum,* N.F., 87(1938):80–84; and Schmid-
Stählin, *op. cit.,* Part I, Vol. I, p. 236. For another view of the
date of the *Homeric Hymn to Apollo,* see Allen and Halliday,
op. cit., 267. (4) An analysis of the use of the digamma in the
Homeric Hymns shows that the *Hymn to Hermes* is much later
than the other three long hymns; see Allen and Halliday, *op.
cit.,* cvi.

Allen and Halliday (*op. cit.,* 275–276) date the *Hymn* to the
seventh century. Their only positive argument is that the
Triphylian or Alphean Pylos, which is where Hermes concealed
the cattle, had disappeared from memory by the end of the
seventh century. This argument is worthless. The geography of
the *Hymn* is derived from Homer; cf. *Iliad,* 2.591–592; 5.545;
11.712.

APPENDICES

APPENDIX

A

HERMES' CATTLE THEFT IN THE HESIODIC *MEGALAI EOIAI*

The Hesiodic *Megalai Eoiai* tell how Hermes stole some cattle from Apollo. Although attributed by the ancients to Hesiod, the *Megalai Eoiai* are regarded by modern scholars as a compilation of fragments composed at different dates, the latest of which are ascribed to the sixth century B.C. Since we have dated the *Homeric Hymn to Hermes* to the end of the sixth century, the *Megalai Eoiai* fragment can safely be said to be earlier than the *Hymn*. In all probability the story in the *Megalai Eoiai* was the point of departure for the further development of the myth by Alcaeus and the author of the *Homeric Hymn to Hermes*. Unfortunately all that has survived of this part of the *Megalai Eoiai* is a paraphrase by the late-Hellenistic mythographer Antoninus Liberalis—a paraphrase not based directly on the *Megalai Eoiai* themselves, but on a version by the Hellenistic poet Nicander. Neverthe-

less a comparison between Antoninus Liberalis and the
Homeric Hymn to Hermes makes it possible to draw a
few conclusions about the relation between the *Hymn*
and the *Megalai Eoiai*.[1]

Antoninus Liberalis says that when Apollo was in
Thessaly, in love with Hymenaeus, grandson of Admetus, Hermes stole a herd of Apollo's cattle which
were grazing in the same place as the cattle of Admetus. Hermes drove the cattle south to the Peloponnese, then westward through the Peloponnese until he
came to the mountainous region of Arcadia. There he
was seen by a man called Battos, who demanded and
received a reward in return for keeping silent about
what he had seen. After Hermes had hidden the cattle
on the west coast of the Peloponnese, he wanted to test
the loyalty of Battos; so he disguised himself and came
to Battos, and offered him a reward for information
on some stolen cattle. Battos accepted the reward
and gave the information, whereupon Hermes, an-
gered by this duplicity, struck him with his wand and
changed him into the rocks that bear his name—the
"watch-posts of Battos."

In Antoninus Liberalis, Hermes and Apollo are not
brought face to face; there is no altercation, no judgment of Zeus, no reconciliation, no mention of the lyre,
which is indispensable to the reconciliation staged in
the *Hymn*. Instead, Antoninus' story focuses its attention on Battos, the informer; for the development of
his plot it is virtually of no consequence whose cattle

---

[1] Antoninus Liberalis, *Metamorphoses*, 23 (Hesiod, Frg. 153,
ed. Rzach). On the date of the *Megalai Eoiai*, see Schmid-
Stählin, *Geschichte der griechischen Literatur*, Part I, Vol. I,
pp. 268–269. The best discussion of the various versions of the
story which are ultimately derived from the *Megalai Eoiai*, and
of their relation to the *Hymn* and versions based on the *Hymn*,
is Holland's "Battos," *Rheinisches Museum*, 75 (1926): 156–
183. This Appendix covers the main points on which I disagree
with him.

Hermes had stolen. There is no reason to doubt that
the version in the *Megalai Eoiai* had the same emphasis—so markedly at variance with the *Homeric Hymn*
—as Antoninus' story. The distinctive feature of the
later development of the myth as reflected in Alcaeus
and the *Homeric Hymn* is the elaboration of the idea
of conflict between Hermes and Apollo.

The informer, whose role is central in the *Megalai
Eoiai*, appears in the *Hymn* also, as a nameless old
man living in Onchestos in Boeotia. But Hermes makes
no covenant with him: he only advises him to hold his
tongue; he does not revisit him nor punish him. The
role of the old man of Onchestos in the *Hymn* is clearly
a traditional element of story which the author
does not trouble to develop fully. Since the episode is
not self-explanatory, the *Hymn's* version of the story
must be the later one.[2]

Antoninus places the scene of the theft in Thessaly,
and motivates Apollo's presence there by his love for
Hymenaeus, the grandson of Admetus. In the *Hymn*
the scene of the theft is the region of Mount Olympus
in Pieria, where all the gods have herds grazing. It is
legitimate to assume that the original authority for
placing the theft in Thessaly was the *Megalai Eoiai*. It
is impossible, however, to attribute to the *Megalai
Eoiai* Antoninus' motivation for Apollo's presence in
Thessaly. Apollo's love for Hymenaeus is a variant of
the erotic motivation for his servitude to Admetus, and
this was an invention of the Hellenistic poet Rhianus.
We can only conclude that the *Megalai Eoiai* placed

[2] Holland (*op. cit.*, 173–175) believes the *Hymn* to be earlier
than the Hesiodic version, but assigns no specific date to either.
His argument is that the greater prominence of the fabulous
element in the *Hymn* points to a more primitive age—a dubious
inference resting on the questionable assumption that the atmosphere and details of Antoninus' story are true to the Hesiodic original.

the theft of the cattle in Thessaly because it took place
during Apollo's period of servitude to Admetus.[3]

Hesiod in the *Eoiai* told of Apollo's servitude to
Admetus as an epilogue to the story of Koronis. I
think it can be demonstrated that it was as an epilogue to the story of Koronis that Hermes' theft was
narrated in the *Megalai Eoiai*. In the first place, the
Eoiai and *Megalai Eoiai* are catalogues of heroines;
to what heroine was the story of the cattle theft attached? It cannot have been Maia, because she was a
goddess, not a heroine. The family of Battos will not
provide an answer because he is merely a folk-tale
figure—his name means "the talker"—and has no
heroic genealogy. We must therefore look for a heroine whose connection with the story is not through
Hermes or Battos, but through Apollo; this can only
be Koronis.[4] In the second place, if Hermes' theft was

---

[3] *Hymn,* 70–71. On Rhianus' version, see scholiast on Euripides, *Alcestis,* 1. In line 70 of the *Hymn* Allen and Halliday
(*The Homeric Hymns,* 273) suggest reading Πηρείης for Πιερίης,
so as to make the *Hymn* consistent with Antoninus, Pereia being
in Thessaly. This would be a mistake: the *Hymn* refers to the
Pieria which is near Olympus (Hesiod, *Theogony,* 53–62), as
is clear from the phrase θεῶν ὄρεα σκιόεντα.

[4] On the form of the *Eoiai* and *Megalai Eoiai,* see Rzach, in
Pauly-Wissowa, *s.v.* "Hesiodos," VIII.1203–1204. No objection
to connecting the Battos episode with the Koronis episode can
be made on the ground that our sources attribute the Koronis
episode to the *Eoiai* and the Battos episode to the *Megalai
Eoiai;* we know that in some cases their subject matter over-
lapped; see Rzach, *loc. cit.* On the character of Battos, see Holland, *op. cit.,* 175–178. Lactantius Placidus (*Metamorphoseon
Narrationes,* II.11) refers to Battos as "the son of Neleus"; this
genealogy, based on the Messenian location of the story in
Ovid, is sufficient indication that Battos had no genuine genealogy. Holland (*loc. cit.*) speculates on a connection with the
Battos of Cyrene, and even with the Cyrene *Eoie;* but he gives
no argument against the more natural hypothesis that the name
Battos was originally Peloponnesian, and he ignores the connec-
tion, through Admetus, with the Koronis *Eoie.* On the latter, see
Hesiod, Frgs. 122–127 (Rzach), and Wilamowitz, *Isyllos von
Epidaurus,* 58–66. Wilamowitz does not consider the possibility
that Hermes' theft of the cattle belonged to the Koronis *Eoie.*

attached to the Koronis story in the *Megalai Eoiai*, it
would explain why in the *Hymn* Hermes stole only
the cows from Apollo's herd, leaving the bull—a fact
which Apollo himself declares to be highly remarkable.
In the Hesiodic story of Koronis, Apollo made all the
cows doubly fertile.[5] In the third place, there is, I believe, an allusion to Hermes' theft of the cattle in Pindar's version of the story of Koronis, which, as Wilamowitz has shown, is based on the Hesiodic story but
which at the same time engages in sharp polemics
against certain features of it that Pindar found incompatible with his own exalted concept of Apollo. Pindar says, criticizing the Hesiodic version, "No mortal,
no god tricks ($\kappa\lambda\epsilon\pi\tau\epsilon\iota$) him [Apollo] in deed or in intention." The mortal who in the Hesiodic version, but
not in Pindar's version, tricked Apollo was Koronis.
Who can the god be if not the arch-trickster Hermes?
It would then follow that in the Hesiodic version of
the Koronis story, but not in Pindar, Hermes tricked
Apollo; this "trick" could be only the theft of the cattle.[6]

If the *Megalai Eoiai* made Hermes' theft of the cattle an episode in Apollo's period of servitude as herds-
man to Admetus, then it follows that the cattle Hermes
stole did not belong to Apollo, but were the cattle of
Admetus tended by Apollo. Apollo has no cattle of his
own in Homer. He first became a pastoral god in the
myth of his servitude to Admetus; as Callimachus says,
"We also call Phoebus the pastoral god since the time
when by the banks of the Amphryssus he tended the
yoke-mares, aflame with love for the young Admetus."
Antoninus combines the *Hymn's* depiction of the cattle
as the property of Apollo with the *Megalai Eoiai's* location of the story in Thessaly; he introduces Apollo's

---

[5] *Hymn*, 196; Callimachus, *Hymns*, II.54; Euripides, *Alcestis*,
569–590.
[6] Pindar, *Pythian*, III.29–30; Wilamowitz, *Isyllos von Epidaurus*, 58–61.

love for Hymenaeus to supply a motivation for his
presence in Thessaly other than his servitude to Admetus. At the same time Antoninus adds that Apollo's
cattle were grazing where the herds of Admetus were;
this addition indicates that in his sources there was
some confusion between Apollo's herd and Admetus'
herd. Two other Hellenistic versions of Hermes' theft
refer to the cattle only as "the cattle tended by Apollo."
The version in Ovid's *Metamorphoses* clearly gives us
to understand that they were the cattle of Admetus
tended by Apollo.[7]

Thus the notion of Hermes invading Apollo's property is one of the novelties in the myth as it developed
after the *Megalai Eoiai*. In the new form of the myth
which culminates in the *Homeric Hymn to Hermes*,
the ownership of the cattle is transferred from Admetus to Apollo, and the scene is transferred to the
region of Mount Olympus, where, according to the
Hymn, all the gods have herds grazing. The myth is
transformed into a study of the competition between
the two gods for property and status.

It can also be shown that the other distinctive feature of the myth in the *Hymn*—the representation of
the thief as a newborn baby—is likewise a novelty introduced after the *Megalai Eoiai*. Hermes is represented as a baby in the *Homeric Hymn*, in Alcaeus'
hymn, on the Caeretan Hydria, and on the Brygos

[7] Callimachus, *Hymns*, II.47–49 (cf. Vergil, *Georgics*, III.2;
Lucan, *Pharsalia*, VI.368); Apollodorus, *Bibliotheca*, III.10.2;
the hypothesis to Pindar's *Pythian Odes*, quoted by Allen and
Halliday, *op. cit.*, 272; Ovid, *Metamorphoses*, II.689–707 (cf.
M. Haupt, *Die Metamorphosen des P. Ovidius Naso*, 8th ed.,
Berlin, 1903, I, 106). Lactantius Placidus (*Metamorphoseon
Narrationes*, II.11) explicitly attributes the ownership of the
cattle to Admetus. Although I have not found the point fully
argued elsewhere, it has often been supposed that the cattle did
originally belong to Admetus; see Kuiper, "De discrepantiis
Hymni Homerici in Mercurium," *Mnemosyne*, n.s., 38(1910):
26, 33–36, and Gruppe, *Griechische Mythologie und Religionsgeschichte*, Vol. II, p. 1327, note 2.

vase. In the separate line of descent which runs from the *Megalai Eoiai* through Nicander to Ovid and Antoninus Liberalis, Hermes is full-grown. The fact that these writers represent Hermes as full-grown, despite the obvious advantages, from the point of view of comedy, of representing him as a baby, shows that they must be following a version which had prestige and authority equal to that of the *Hymn;* this source can be only the *Megalai Eoiai.*[8]

[8] Holland, *op. cit.,* 159.

APPENDIX

B

THE TEXT OF
THE *HOMERIC*
HYMN TO HERMES

THE ARGUMENTS FOR ITS UNITY

The most important argument for the thesis that lines
513–580 of the *Hymn* were not written by the author
of lines 1–512 is the difference in religious attitudes
and conceptions between the two parts.[1] Here I wish
to consider only the arguments which the editors of the
Oxford (Allen and Halliday) edition advance in defense of the unity of the *Hymn*.[2] They are the only
modern editors to take this point of view.

They seem to believe that the only argument for
separating lines 513–580 rests on a mistranslation of
line 533.[3] This is to ignore numerous other disjunctions
and inconsistencies. On the contrast in style, Radermacher and Humbert may be consulted;[4] the difference appears to me to be self-evident. On the construc-

[1] See above, Chapter 5.
[2] Allen and Halliday, 340–341, 344.
[3] *Ibid.*, 344.
[4] Radermacher, *Der Homerische Hermeshymnus*, 161–171;
Humbert, *Homère Hymnes*, 110–111.

tion of lines 1–512 as a dramatic unity Radermacher gives an admirable analysis;[5] in contrast with the tight construction of lines 1–512, neither of the chief topics of lines 513–580—the magic wand and Hermes' claims in the sphere of prophecy—connects with anything in the first part of the *Hymn*. The inconsistencies in detail include the following: (1) lines 574–575 duplicate the ending formula of lines 506–508: "They both were friends ever after"; (2) the friendship "lasting to this day" of lines 506–508 is rudely ignored in lines 514–515, where Apollo expresses fear of losing the lyre and his bow; (3) particularly incoherent is Apollo's fear for the lyre, which in line 509 is the gift that *proves* Hermes' friendship for Apollo; (4) in line 529 Apollo gives Hermes the magic wand which was already his in line 210; (5) the placing of Hermes in charge of oxen in line 567 repeats the event of line 498.

The much-discussed line 533 reads, in the Oxford text, μαντείην δὲ φέριστε διοτρεφὲς ἣν ἐρεείνεις. Groddeck, who first argued for the separation of lines 513–580, translated ἐρεείνεις as "demand" and pointed out that Hermes had made no previous demands for prophecy. The Oxford editors make much of their contention that the word means not "demand" but "ask about," "mention." Hermes mentioned prophecy in line 471, they say, and here is the reply.[6] Radermacher has rightly replied that the word always implies a question, and that when it may be translated "mention" it means "mention questioningly"; but in line 471 all Hermes says is, "You, Apollo, have been given charge of prophecy by Zeus."[7] Quite apart from the meaning of ἐρεείνεις, it is absurd to regard line 471 as justifying a fifteen-line speech from Apollo explaining why Her-

[5] Radermacher, *op. cit.*, 213–218.
[6] Allen and Halliday, 344.
[7] Radermacher, "Zum Homerischen Hermeshymnos," *Classical Quarterly* 27(1933):156–157.

mes cannot receive the gift of prophecy. Furthermore, the Oxford editors have, without any discussion, adopted the weaker manuscript reading in line
533, when the stronger reading makes the line utterly
and unquestionably inconsistent with lines 1–512. The
best manuscript (M) reads διαμπερὲς, not διοτρεφὲς. The
reading of M is preferable because (1) while it is easy
to see why διαμπερὲς should have been changed to
διοτρεφὲς to make the line consistent with the rest of
the *Hymn*, no reason can be given for the reverse; and
(2) διοτρεφὲς repeats φέριστε. But of course there has
been no "continual mentioning," much less "continual
questioning" about prophecy.

The Oxford editors ask, "What do we know of the
'unities' of the seventh century?" [8] If such a position is
taken seriously, it is nothing but an appeal to abandon
the effort to understand the mind of the author rather
than abandon faith in the unity of the *Hymn*. Ask no
questions, we are told—in the seventh century all
things are possible; any other attitude is "subjective
prepossession." [9]

TWO READINGS THAT FOLLOW FROM
THE SEPARATION OF LINES 513–580

Line 533.—The Oxford text reads μαντείην δὲ φέριστε
διοτρεφὲς ἦν ἐρεείνεις. M's διαμπερὲς is preferable to διοτρεφὲς.[10]

Line 515.—The Oxford text reads μή μοι ἀνακλέψῃς
κίθαριν καὶ καμπύλα τόξα. M's ἅμα κλέψῃς is preferable because (1) the effort to make lines 513–580 consistent
with lines 1–512 is a mistaken one; (2) ἀνακλέψῃς im-

[8] Allen and Halliday, 341.
[9] *Ibid.*
[10] See above; cf. Radermacher, *Homerische Hermeshymnus*,
166–167.

plies that Hermes once had Apollo's bow; (3) ἅμα κλέψῃς places the Apolline reviser on the side of the rival tradition which regarded the *citharis* as Apollo's from the start;[11] (4) the line is based on line 131 of the *Hymn to Apollo*, where the *citharis* is regarded as Apollo's aboriginal instrument.[12]

ONE READING RELATED TO THE INTERPRETATION OF THE EXCHANGE SCENE

Lines 503–504.—The Oxford text reads Ἔνθα βόες μὲν ἔπειτ ποτί δάθεον λειμῶνα / ἐτραπέτην. The best manuscript, M, reads βόας. The Oxford editors say that βόες gives a "stronger sense"; the cows went home of themselves, as to the troughs in line 103. The sense is so strong as to be absurd. It is one thing for cows to go voluntarily to the feeding troughs; it is quite another for them to go voluntarily from Elis to Pieria. It is better to take Hermes and Apollo as the subject of the verb, and read βόας, since the exchange scene establishes joint patronage by both gods over cattle,[13] and since the sentence is linked to line 506, where both gods are said to amuse themselves with the lyre.

SUGGESTED EMENDATIONS

Lines 414–417.—The Oxford text reads

τότε δὴ κρατὺς Ἀργειφόντης

χῶρον ὑποβλήδην ἐσκέψατο πῦρ ἀμαρύσσων

. . . .

[11] See above, Chapter 5, pages 95–99.
[12] See Radermacher, *Homerische Hermeshymnus*, 161–162.
[13] See above, Chapter 5, pages 90–92.

ἐγκρύψαι μεμαώς· Λητοῦς δ' ἐρικυδέος υἱὸν

ῥεῖα μάλ' ἐπρήϋνεν ἑκηβόλον, ὡς ἔθελ' αὐτός,

Radermacher maintains that Hermes wanted to hide
the lyre, which he thinks was mentioned in the lacuna
after line 415.[14] But why should Hermes want to hide
the lyre? Radermacher himself points out that Hermes
is the aggressor throughout; the Oxford editors have
proved that all Apollo had tried to do was to lead away
his own cattle; it is Hermes' idea to show off the lyre so
as to effect an exchange.[15] Furthermore, if it were the
lyre, then, with Radermacher, we shall have to place
another lacuna after line 416, where it must have been
stated that Apollo saw Hermes trying to hide the lyre,
and demanded an explanation. Apart from the objection to increasing the number of lacunae, this would
spoil the surprise in Hermes' ensuing revelation of the
lyre.

The Oxford editors say that Hermes tried to hide the
pieces of meat mentioned in lines 135–136.[16] But since
the skins have already been discovered (lines 403–
404), what is the point of hiding the meat? And why
does not the *Hymn* go on to tell us whether he did actually hide the meat? What is the logical connection between wanting to hide the meat and actually proceed-
ing to produce the lyre? Even if there is a satisfactory
answer to these questions, we shall have to place another lacuna after line 416, where the necessary explanations were supplied.

It is hard to imagine anything that Hermes should
want to hide; ἐγκρύψαι is therefore suspect. I suggest
reading, without a lacuna between lines 415 and 416,

14 Radermacher, *Homerische Hermeshymnus*, 147–148.
15 Allen and Halliday, 330–332. See above, Chapter 5, pp.
90–93.
16 Allen and Halliday, 332.

ἐκκλέψαι μεμαὼς Λητοῦς ἐρικυδέος υἱόν.

ῥεῖα μάλ' ἐπρήϋνεν ἐκηβόλον, ὡς ἔθελ' αὐτός,

"Then the strong Slayer of Argus looked askance over the place with fire-darting eyes, intent on cheating the son of glorious Leto. Easily he soothed the Far-darter, just as he wanted." For ἐκκλέπτειν in this sense, compare Sophocles, *Philoctetes*, 968 and 56, and *Trachiniae*, 437. The tricking referred to is his contemplated shrewd bargain (cf. μῦθοι κερδαλέοι in line 463), which was led up to by his producing the lyre in line 418, and which he had in mind as far back as lines 410–413, when he "froze" the cattle. When he looks over the place in line 415, he is not seeking a place to hide something, but a position for playing the lyre—cf. lines 424 and 425,

στῆ ῥ'ὅ γε θαρσήσας ἐπ' ἀριστερὰ Μαιάδος υἱὸς

Φοίβου Ἀπόλλωνος,

Misinterpretation of the χῶρον in line 415 favored the substitution of ἐγκρύψαι for ἐκκλέψαι. Then the punctuation was disturbed, and δέ was inserted after Λητοῦς. The emendation is not drastic, and is compensated for by the fact that it gets rid of the lacuna.

Lines 418–420.—The text of the Oxford edition reads

λαβὼν δ' ἐπ' ἀριστερὰ χειρὸς

πλήκτρῳ ἐπειρήτιζε κατὰ μέλος· ἡ δ'ὑπὸ χειρὸς

σμερδαλέον κονάβησε,

In line 419, ἡ (i.e., λύρη) lacks an antecedent. I agree with the Oxford editors that the lyre was not men-

tioned in a lacuna after line 415.[17] The Oxford editors
note that M reads λύρην instead of χειρὸς in line 419,
where it is of course unmetrical. They therefore suggest ἐπ᾿ ἀριστέρ᾿ ἄθυρμα, regarding M's λύρην as a gloss,
and χειρὸς in line 418 as an intrusion from line 419.[18] But
ἄθυρμα is very awkward for the first mention of the
lyre in this context, and supplies a poor antecedent to
ἥ. I suggest reading λύρην δ᾿ ἐπ᾿ ἀριστέρ᾿ ἀείρας. When
χειρὸς displaced ἀείρας, λαβών, perhaps a gloss indicating
the original presence of ἀείρας, displaced λύρην.

   Lines 471–474.—The Oxford text reads

   καὶ τιμὰς σὲ δέ φασι δαήμεναι ἐκ Διὸς ὀμφῆς

   μαντείας θ᾿ Ἑκάεργε Διὸς πάρα, θέσφατα πάντα.

   τῶν νῦν αὐτὸς ἔγωγε †παῖδ᾿ ἀφνειὸν† δεδάηκα.

   σοὶ δ᾿ αὐτάγρετόν ἐστι δαήμεναι ὅττι μενοινᾷς.

If in line 473 we accept Allen's excellent conjecture of
πεδάφνειον (for μετάφνειον), we get the sense, "I have
recently learned about them," i.e., about Apollo's prophetic powers. But when did Hermes learn about
Apollo's prophetic powers? It is very forced to see an
allusion to line 212; the bird was not the important
informer, but rather the old man of Onchestos. Much
better sense is gained by a simple change in punctuation:

   τῶν νῦν αὐτὸς ἔγωγε πεδάφνειον δεδάηκα,

   σοὶ δ᾿ αὐτάγρετόν ἐστι δαήμεναι ὅττι μενοινᾷς.

"But of the things which I have recently discovered"
—i.e., the art of the lyre—"you are free to learn what

---

[17] See above, pages 151–152.
[18] *Ibid.*, 332–333.

you will." Hermes says he is willing to be to Apollo in
the matter of the lyre what Zeus is to Apollo in the
matter of prophecy—a typically impudent statement
for Hermes to make.

BIBLIOGRAPHY

BIBLIOGRAPHY

BOOKS AND ARTICLES

ALLEN, T. W., W. R. HALLIDAY, and E. E. SIKES. *The Homeric Hymns*, 2d ed. Oxford, 1936.

AMIRA, K. VON. *Der Stab in der germanischen Rechtsymbolik* (*Abhandlungen der Königlich Bayerischen Akademie der Wissenschaften, Philosophisch-philologische und historische Klasse*, Vol. 25, No. 1). Munich, 1909.

BEAZLEY, J. D. *Attic Red-Figure Vase-Painters*. Oxford, 1942.

BIZARD, L. "Inscriptions du Ptoion. 2. Les Pisistratides au sanctuaire." *Bulletin de correspondance hellénique*, 44(1920): 237–241.

BLOOMFIELD, M. "The Art of Stealing in Hindu Fiction." *American Journal of Philology*, 44(1923):97–133.

BOETTCHER, R. *De Hymno in Mercurium Homerico*. Halle, 1906.

BOLTE, J., and G. POLÍVKA. *Anmerkungen zu den Kinder- und Hausmärchen der Brüder Grimm*. 3 vols. Leipzig, 1913–18.

BOWRA, C. M. *Greek Lyric Poetry*. Oxford, 1936.

BRIFFAULT, R. *The Mothers*. 3 vols. New York, 1927.

BUCHHOLZ, E. *Die Homerischen Realien*. 3 vols. Leipzig, 1871–1884.

BUSOLT, G., and H. SWOBODA. *Griechische Staatskunde*. 2 vols. Munich, 1920, 1926.

CALHOUN, G. M. "Homer's Gods: Myth and Märchen." *American Journal of Philology*, 60(1939):1–28.

——— "The Higher Criticism on Olympus." *American Journal of Philology*, 58(1937):257–274.

CHARBONNEAUX, J. "Tholos et Prytanée." *Bulletin de correspondance hellénique*, 49(1925):158–178.

CORNELIUS, F. *Die Tyrannis in Athen*. Munich, 1929.

CROME, J. F. "Hipparcheioi Hermai." *Mitteilungen des deutschen archäologischen Instituts, Athenische Abteilung,* 60–61 (1935–36): 300–313.

———— "Kerykeia." *Mitteilungen des deutschen archäologischen Instituts, Athenische Abteilung,* 63(1938):117–126.

DEUBNER, L. *Attische Feste.* Berlin, 1932.

———— "Die viersaitige Leier." *Mitteilungen des deutschen archäologischen Instituts, Athenische Abteilung,* 54(1929): 194–200.

DOMASZEWSKI, A. VON. *Die Hermen der Agora zu Athen (Sitzungsberichte der Heidelberger Akademie der Wissenschaften, Philosophisch-historische Klasse,* 5[1914], Abh. 10).

DORNSEIFF, F. "Zum Homerischen Hermeshymnos." *Rheinisches Museum für Philologie,* N.F., 87(1938):80–84.

EITREM, S. "Der Homerische Hymnus an Hermes." *Philologus,* 65(1906):248–282.

———— "De Mercurio Aristophaneo." *Philologus,* 68(1909): 344–367.

FARNELL, L. R. *Cults of the Greek States.* 5 vols. Oxford, 1896–1909.

————, trans. *Works of Pindar.* 3 vols. London, 1930–32.

FRAZER, J. G. *The Magic Art and the Evolution of Kings (The Golden Bough,* 3d ed., Vols. 1, 2). London, 1911.

———— *Taboo and the Perils of the Soul (The Golden Bough,* 3d ed., Vol. 3). London, 1911.

GERNET, L., and A. BOULANGER. *Le Génie grec dans la religion.* Paris, 1932.

GIRARD, P. "Le Mythe de Pandore dans la poésie hésiodique." *Revue des études grecques,* 22(1909):217–230.

GLOTZ, G. *The Aegean Civilization.* New York, 1925.

———— *Ancient Greece at Work.* New York, 1926.

———— *La Solidarité de la famille dans le droit criminel en Grèce.* Paris, 1904.

GOLDMAN, H. "The Origin of the Greek Herm." *American Journal of Archaeology,* 46(1942):58–68.

GOW, A. S. F. "Elpis and Pandora." *Essays and Studies Presented to William Ridgeway,* edited by E. C. Quiggin, pp. 99–109. Cambridge, 1914.

GRIERSON, P. J. H. *The Silent Trade.* Edinburgh, 1903.

GRUPPE, O. *Griechische Mythologie und Religionsgeschichte.* 2 vols. Munich, 1906.

GUARDUCCI, M. "Leggende dell' antica Grecia relative all' origine dell' umanità." *Memorie della reala Accademia nazionale dei Lincei, classe di scienze morali storiche e filologiche,* 2(1926):377–460.

GUILLEMIN, M., and J. DUCHESNE. "Sur l'origine asiatique de la cithare grecque." *L'Antiquité classique*, 4(1935):117–124.

HARRISON, JANE. "Pandora's Box." *Journal of Hellenic Studies*, 20(1900):99–114.

———— *Prolegomena to the Study of Greek Religion*, 2d ed. Cambridge, 1906.

HEADLAM, W. "Prometheus and the Garden of Eden." *Classical Quarterly*, 28(1934):63–71.

HEICHELHEIM, F. *Wirtschaftsgeschichte des Altertums*. 2 vols. Leiden, 1938.

HIRZEL, R. *Der Eid*. Leipzig, 1902.

———— *Themis, Dike und Verwandtes*. Leipzig, 1907.

HOLLAND, R. "Battos." *Rheinisches Museum für Philologie*, 75 (1926):156–183.

HOYT, E. E. *Primitive Trade, Its Psychology and Economics*. London, 1920.

HUMBERT, J. *Homère Hymnes*, Budé edition. Paris, 1936.

JAEGER, W. *Paideia: The Ideals of Greek Culture*. Oxford, 1939.

JEVONS, F. B. "Graeco-Italian Magic." *Anthropology and the Classics*, edited by R. R. Marett. Oxford, 1907.

DE JOSSELIN DE JONG, J. P. B. "De oorsprong van den goddelijken bedrieger." *Mededeelingen der koninklijke Akademie van wetenschappen, Amsterdam, Afdeeling Letterkunde*, Deel. 68, Serie B (1929):1–30.

JUDEICH, W. *Topographie von Athen*, 2d ed. Munich, 1931.

KERN, O. *Die Religion der Griechen*. 3 vols. Berlin, 1926–38.

KRAIKER, W. "Epiktetos." *Jahrbuch des deutschen archäologischen Instituts*, 44(1929):141–197.

KRISTENSEN, W. B. "De goddelijke bedrieger." *Mededeelingen der koninklijke Akademie van wetenschappen, Amsterdam, Afdeeling Letterkunde*, Deel. 66, Serie B (1927–28):63–88.

KUIPER, K. "De discrepantiis Hymni Homerici in Mercurium." *Mnemosyne*, n.s., 38(1910):1–50.

LANG, A. *The Homeric Hymns*. New York, 1899.

LANGLOTZ, E. "Epimetheus." *Die Antike*, 6(1930):1–14.

LATTE, K. *Heiliges Recht: Untersuchungen zur Geschichte der sakralen Rechtsformen in Griechenland*. Tübingen, 1920.

LAUM, B. *Heiliges Geld*. Tübingen, 1924.

MAINE, H. S. *Village Communities in the East and West*. New York, 1880.

MALINOWSKI, B. *Myth in Primitive Psychology*. New York, 1926.

———— *The Sexual Life of Savages in North-Western Melanesia*. London, 1929.

MARETT, R. R. *Head, Heart, and Hands in Human Evolution*. London, 1935.

MEYER, E. "Hesiods Erga und das Gedicht von den fünf Menschengeschlechtern." *Kleine Schriften*, II, 15–16. Halle, 1924.

MURRAY, G. *Five Stages of Greek Religion*. New York, 1925.

NÄGELSBACH, C. F. VON. *Homerische Theologie*, 3d ed., Nuremberg, 1884.

NILSSON, M. P. *Greek Popular Religion*. New York, 1940.

——— *Griechische Feste*. Leipzig, 1906.

——— *A History of Greek Religion*. Oxford, 1925.

——— *Homer and Mycenae*. London, 1933.

——— *Minoan-Mycenaean Religion and Its Survival in Greek Religion*. Lund, 1927.

——— *The Mycenaean Origin of Greek Mythology*. Berkeley, 1932.

OVERBECK, J. *Griechische Kunstmythologie*, Vol. 3, Bk. 5 (Apollo). Leipzig, 1887.

PARKE, H. W. *History of the Delphic Oracle*. Oxford, 1939.

PRELLER, L. *Griechische Mythologie*, 4th ed., revised by C. Robert. 2 vols. Berlin, 1894.

RADERMACHER, L. *Der Homerische Hermeshymnus* (*Sitzungsberichte der Akademie der Wissenschaften in Wien, Philosophisch-historische Klasse*, Vol. 213, Part 1). 1933.

RAINGEARD, P. *Hermès psychagogue: Essai sur les origines du culte d'Hermès*. Paris, 1936.

REINACH, S. *Répertoire des vases peints grecs et étrusques*. 2 vols. Paris, 1899, 1900.

ROBERT, C. "Pandora." *Hermes*, 49(1914):17–38.

——— "Zum Homerischen Hermeshymnos." *Hermes*, 41 (1906):389–425.

ROSE, H. J. *A Handbook of Greek Mythology*. New York, 1928.

——— *Primitive Culture in Greece*. London, 1925.

RZACH, A. "Bericht über die Publikationen zu Hesiodos für das Jahrzehnt 1909–18." *Jahresbericht über die Fortschritte der klassischen Altertumswissenschaft*, 119(1924):1–115.

SCHMID, W., and O. STÄHLIN. *Geschichte der griechischen Literatur*, Part I. Munich, 1929.

SCHRADER, O. *Sprachvergleichung und Urgeschichte*. Jena, 1906.

SCHWARTZ, E. "Prometheus bei Hesiod." *Sitzungsberichte der Königlich Preussischen Akademie der Wissenschaften*, Berlin, 1915, pp. 133–148.

SOLDERS, S. *Die ausserstädtische Kulte und die Einigung Attikas*. Lund, 1931.

THOMPSON, H. A. *The Tholos of Athens and Its Predecessors* (*Hesperia*, Supp. IV). Baltimore, 1940.

USENER, H. "Psithyros." *Rheinisches Museum für Philologie*, 59(1904):623–624.

DE VRIES, J. *The Problem of Loki (Folklore Fellows Communications,* Vol. 43, No. 110). Helsinki, 1933.

WEBER, L. "Kerameikos-Kulte." *Mitteilungen des deutschen archäologischen Instituts, Athenische Abteilung,* 50(1925):139–156.

WENIGER, L. "Die monatliche Opferung von Olympia." *Klio,* 14(1915):395–446.

———— "Olympische Studien." *Archiv für Religionswissenschaft,* 20(1920–21):41–78.

WILAMOWITZ-MOELLENDORFF, U. von. *Aristoteles und Athen.* 2 vols. Berlin, 1893.

———— *Der Glaube der Hellenen.* 2 vols. Berlin, 1931–32.

———— *Heimkehr des Odysseus.* Berlin, 1927.

———— "Hephaistos." *Nachrichten von der Königlichen Gesellschaft der Wissenschaften zu Göttingen, Philologisch-historische Klasse,* 1895, pp. 217–245.

———— *Hesiodos Erga.* Berlin, 1928.

———— *Isyllos von Epidaurus (Philologische Untersuchungen,* 9). Berlin, 1886.

———— *Pindaros.* Berlin, 1922.

———— *Sappho und Simonides.* Berlin, 1913.

ZIELINSKI, T. *The Religion of Ancient Greece.* Oxford, 1926.

ZSCHIETZSCHMANN, W. "Attische Bildkunst um 560." *Jahrbuch des deutschen archäologischen Instituts,* 46(1931):45–60.

DICTIONARIES AND ENCYCLOPEDIAS

BÄCHTOLD-STÄUBLI, H. *Handwörterbuch des deutschen Aberglaubens.* 8 vols. Berlin, 1927–37.

BOISACQ, E. *Dictionnaire étymologique de la langue grecque,* 3d ed. Heidelberg, 1938.

DAREMBERG, C., and E. SAGLIO. *Dictionnaire des antiquités grecques et romaines.* 5 vols. Paris, 1877–1910.

EBELING, H., ed. *Lexicon Homericum.* Leipzig, 1880–85.

EBERT, M. *Reallexikon der Vorgeschichte.* 15 vols. Berlin, 1924–1932.

Encyclopedia of the Social Sciences, edited by E. R. A. Seligman. 15 vols. New York, 1930–35.

ERNOUT, A., and A. MEILLET. *Dictionnaire étymologique de la langue latine.* Paris, 1932.

HASTINGS, J. *Encyclopedia of Religion and Ethics.* 13 vols. Edinburgh, 1908–26.

LIDDELL, H. G., and R. SCOTT. *A Greek-English Lexicon,* new edition revised by H. S. Jones. Oxford, 1940.

Pauly's Real-Encyclopädie der klassischen Altertumswissenschaft, new edition, edited by G. Wissowa and others. Stuttgart, 1894–   .

ROSCHER, W. H. *Ausführliches Lexikon der griechischen und römischen Mythologie.* 6 vols. Leipzig, 1884–1937.

SCHRADER, O. *Reallexikon der indogermanischen Altertums-kunde,* 2d ed., edited by A. Nehring. 2 vols. Berlin, 1917, 1929.

WALDE, A. *Vergleichendes Wörterbuch der indogermanischen Sprache,* revised by J. Pokorny. 3 vols. Berlin, 1927–32.

INDEX

INDEX

NORMAN O. BROWN was born in 1913 in El Oro, Mexico, where his father was active as a mining engineer. He was educated at Oxford University, the University of Chicago, and the University of Wisconsin, where he took his doctorate in 1942. Following a year spent as Professor of Languages at Nebraska Wesleyan University, he served three years as a research analyst with the Office of Strategic Services. For many years he was Professor of Classics at Wesleyan University, and then taught at the University of Rochester. He is currently Professor of Humanities, Cowell College, University of California at Santa Cruz. He is the author of *Life Against Death: The Psychoanalytical Meaning of History* and *Love's Body* (both are available in Vintage Books).

VINTAGE CRITICISM,
LITERATURE, MUSIC, AND ART

VINTAGE BELLES—LETTRES